Still Growing

Still Growing

The Creative Self in Older Adulthood

Donald Capps

CASCADE *Books* · Eugene, Oregon

STILL GROWING
The Creative Self in Older Adulthood

Cascade Books
An Imprint of Wipf and Stock Publishers
199 W. 8th Ave., Suite 3
Eugene, OR 97401

www.wipfandstock.com

ISBN 13: 978-1-62564-460-2

Cataloging-in-Publication data:

Capps, Donald.

    Still growing : the creative self in older adulthood / Donald Capps.

    xx + 190 p. ; 23 cm. Includes bibliographical references and index.

    ISBN 13: 978-1-62564-460-2

    1. Aging—Religious aspects—Christianity. 2. Older Christians—Religious life.
3. Erikson, Erik H. (Erik Homburger), 1902–1994. 4. Freud, Sigmund, 1856–1939. 5.
James, William, 1842–1910. 6. Snow White and the seven dwarfs (Motion picture).

BV4580 C37 2014

Manufactured in the U.S.A.

To the Memory of Paul W. Pruyser

1916–1987

Contents

Tables

Acknowledgments

I WANT TO THANK the editorial team at Cascade Books for their support, especially K. C. Hanson, editor-in-chief, for his astute editorial observations and suggestions; also Jim Tedrick, managing editor; Matthew Wimer, assistant managing editor; and Laura Poncy, editorial administrator. I would also like to express my appreciation to James Stock, marketing director, and Amanda Wehner, marketing coordinator. Finally, I am grateful to Jeremy Funk, copyeditor, Heather Carraher, typesetter, and Mike Surber, cover designer, for their technical skills and creative acumen.

This book is dedicated to the memory of Paul W. Puyser, whom I came to know as a colleague and friend through our involvement in the Society for the Scientific Study of Religion. When I was serving as the editor of the *Journal for the Scientific Study of Religion,* he sent me a manuscript in October 1986, and in his accompanying note he said that he did not want any special consideration, but he observed that in light of his struggle against cancer, this might well be his "swan song" as far as his work in the psychology of religion was concerned. Sadly, he was right. He died the following April, the victim of a sudden heart attack. His article was titled "Where Do We Go From Here?"[1] I felt at the time that this title was especially fitting, for I could almost hear him asking this question of the universe at the moment of his death, and then, having asked it, adding something like, "But don't tell me. I'll want to see and hear it for myself." If older adulthood begins at seventy, Paul died the very year that he entered this period of his life. But as I hope this book will show, he had already developed a profound understanding of this period in life. His

1. Pruyser, "Where Do We Go From Here?"

xi

writings on the subject were tremendously helpful when, on the brink of
older adulthood, I found myself asking the same question: where do we
go from here?

Introduction

. . . . .

*Grow: to increase in some specified manner; to come to be;
to develop so as to be*

Old: having lived or been in existence for a long time

*Creative: having or showing imagination; employing the
imagination and inventive powers*

*Self: the identity, character, or essential qualities of a
person*

. . . . .

THIS IS A BOOK I never thought I would write, much less discover as I was writing it that I actually enjoyed doing so. I had always thought that growing old would be a rather discouraging subject, and although I have written about discouraging subjects before, I viewed the writing of a book on these subjects as a way to formulate practical strategies for dealing with them so that they would no longer seem discouraging. In other words, these other subjects invited me to identify the grounds for hope that were already present or that might be teased out of them by studying them with more care than I would normally have done.

But the subject of growing old seemed so discouraging that I could not begin to imagine that it could lend itself to the same approach or strategy. In fact, it even occurred to me that one of the reasons we Christians have emphasized our hope in the afterlife is that it provides an invaluable distraction from the discouraging thought of growing old. We can tell ourselves that growing old is an ordeal that we need to suffer through in order to gain entry to heaven, a land of perfect contentment and peace. While I would not wish to minimize in any way the comforting effects of this ultimate hope, it leaves us somewhat in the lurch as we contemplate the intervening years.

It was easy, of course, to tell myself that the prospect of growing old is not nearly as bad as I assumed it to be. I even told myself that there must be something wrong with me for thinking of it this way. But after giving these suggestions some thought, I came to the conclusion that they merely shifted the blame from older adulthood itself to the one who was on the verge of becoming an older adult. So I protested, "It's not my fault. It's the reality of the situation." So much for the well-intentioned attempt to argue myself out of the conviction that older adulthood is an inherently discouraging affair.

So, what to do? I began rereading the writings of a couple authors—Sigmund Freud and William James—who had been of great assistance to me in the past. Specifically, I went back to Freud's book on humor—*Jokes and Their Relation to the Unconscious*—and revisited his idea that humor saves in the expenditure of our not-unlimited psychological resources. Specifically, it enables us to forego our normal tendency to lend ourselves to *painful emotions, costly inhibitions,* and *difficult thinking.*[2] Returning to Freud did not change my view of older adulthood as inherently discouraging, but it did open the door to a more hopeful view by suggesting that I need not waste my own not-unlimited psychological resources on the subject. It was simply not worth having painful emotions about, or trying to say nice things about, or even trying to think about it in a practical or useful way. In effect, Freud's view of what humor does for us gave me all the incentive I needed to *quit* thinking about growing old and the fact that it was happening to me.

On the other hand, Freud's assistance here was mainly helpful in giving me a defensible rationale for avoiding the subject of older adulthood: there are better things to think about. Yet, it wasn't always possible to forget about the fact that I was becoming an *older* adult, especially when there were signs—physical, mental, emotional, and social—that it

2. Freud, *Jokes and Their Relation to the Unconscious,* 293. I present Freud's theory in more detail in chapter 6.

was, as it were, dogging my path. So I needed something more. I found this something more in the writings of William James, especially in "The Energies of Men," his presidential address to the American Philosophical Association given on December 28, 1906. James delivered this address when he was sixty-four years old. It was therefore written in what was for him the twilight of his life, because he was already suffering from heart failure and died four years later at the age of sixty-eight.

In this address he discussed energizing ideas.[3] He noted that some ideas have an inhibiting effect while other ideas can be "energy-releas-ing." Sometimes these energy-releasing ideas are so powerful that they "transfigure" a person's life, "unlocking innumerable powers which, but for the idea, would never have come into play."[4]

On the one hand, an energizing idea can be an idea that we have known about for a long time and perhaps even embraced at an earlier stage in life, but that we now experience as genuinely life-changing. In his *The Varieties of Religious Experience*, written in 1901–1902, James had suggested that religious conversions are often the result of a idea that one has known about but that suddenly forces itself upon oneself and causes one to look at life—especially one's own—in an entirely new way. In effect, this idea recrystallizes one's whole system of thought.[5] Other people, of course, may wonder why this idea has had such a monumental effect on this person. They may say, "It's not a new idea at all," or, "It's hardly earthshaking." But for this particular individual it *is* strikingly new and it *is* earthshaking.

On the other hand, an energizing idea can be a brand-new idea, the sort of idea that when *it comes* to us—which is how we think of its occurrence—we say to ourselves, "I never thought of it that way before." In any event, this is the new idea that occurred to me: I had been using the phrase *growing old* in a very negative way because my focus was on the word *old*. But then I began to shift my attention to the word *growing*, and it suddenly occurred to me that *growing* in the context in which I was using the phrase *growing old* is a very positive word. As one of the definitions cited at the beginning of this introduction indicates, *to grow* means "to develop so as to be." One *could* take this to mean only that one is simply developing into something old. But, if so, there is a certain

3. James, "The Energies of Men," 1236–39.

4. Ibid., 1236.

5. James, *The Varieties of Religious Experience*, 183–84.

paradox in this regard, for *old* is defined as something that has "lived or been in existence for a long time." How can something suddenly come to be when it has been in existence for a long time?

Instead, I began to center my attention on the word *growing* and to think seriously about the fact that older adulthood is a period of growth. This became the energizing idea that fundamentally changed my way of viewing the experience of growing old. Older adulthood is often viewed as a period of decline, if not of deterioration; but there is no reason for us *not* to view it as a period of growth and development. In thinking of it this way, I recalled a passage in James's book *Pragmatism,* published in 1907, in which he referred to "the letting loose of hope."[6]

There are many reasons why this idea had not occurred to me before. One is that I simply assumed that older adulthood is a time of dissolution, decrepitude, and decay. To be sure, I knew older persons who appeared to be vital and even full of life, but I could not help thinking that this very vitality disguises the fact that they are in a period of their lives when the very opposite of growth is occurring. The thesaurus says that antonyms of *growing* are "lessening," "shrinking" and "withering."[7] I was also mindful of the fact that we tend to praise older persons who grow old "gracefully." The qualifying word *graceful* is rarely used in reference to the growth that children, adolescents, and younger adults experience. In fact, we tend to view the growth of adolescents as anything but graceful. Why do we use the word *graceful* in relation to older adults? This is probably because we do not think of older adulthood as a period of growth but as a period of lessening, shrinking, and withering—in other words, the very opposite of growth, and we think that some older persons accept this diminution more gracefully than others do.

The fact that older adulthood is a period of growth and development is the potentially energizing idea that informs this book. No doubt, some readers will question whether this idea can be genuinely energizing. They may think it is interesting enough but hardly the kind of idea that releases energies. They may even feel that the idea that older adulthood is a period of growth and development is an expression of desperation or even of denial, a refusal to acknowledge that the author is getting on in years. Of course, they may be right, but the very purpose of this book is to make a case for this idea and its potential for changing one's view of older

6. James, *Pragmatism,* 49.

7. Agnes et al., eds., *Webster's New World Roget's A–Z Thesaurus,* 354.

adulthood from one of discouragement to hope. Moreover, this book is intended to show that this idea is fundamentally true, for the more this energizing idea took hold of me, the more aware I became that in my own life and in the lives of older persons I know, growth and development are the norm. It's just that I wasn't really noticing that this is, in fact, the case. To be sure, there is also evidence of the fact that we are experiencing growing pains, a term usually applied to young children and used, as the dictionary reminds us, rather loosely and with no precise medical meaning.[8] But calling the experiences of older adulthood growing pains is very different from declaring that older adulthood is a period of lessening, shrinking, and withering.

Having said what this book is essentially about, I would now like to comment briefly on the way that it is structured. Part 1 focuses on the transition to older adulthood, and it is largely autobiographical. Chapter 1 relates my decision to embrace older adulthood, while chapter 2 concerns my reunion with my boyhood self and his continuing assistance in navigating this new terrain. There are, of course, many other resources that one is likely to draw upon in the transition to older adulthood, but these chapters serve as an invitation to readers to recognize that they themselves possess inner resources of which they may not be fully aware.

Part 2 is concerned to make the case that growth and development are integral to older adulthood. Building on Erik H. Erikson's life-cycle model,[9] chapter 3 presents my proposal that older adulthood consists of at least three developmental stages, each of them about a decade in length or duration, and chapter 4 presents the view of Paul W. Pruyser that the aging process is one of forward movement.[10] The fact that chapter 5, the culminating chapter in this section of the book, focuses on his article about creativity in older adulthood[11] is the basis for the book's subtitle—*The Creative Self in Older Adulthood*. Creativity is itself a sign of growth, and it seems to be at the center of the growth that occurs in older adulthood. Creativity, after all, requires imagination and inventiveness in light of changing circumstances, and these capacities typically derive from the playfulness, the curiosity, and the pleasure-seeking that older adults share with children.

8. Agnes et al., eds., *Webster's New World College Dictionary*, 629.

9. Erikson, *Childhood and Society* (1st ed.), chap. 7; Erikson, *Identity and the Life Cycle*, chapter 2.

10. Pruyser, "Aging."

11. Pruyser, "Creativity in Aging Persons."

To illustrate the creativity of older adults, the final chapter of part 2 focuses on artists who in their later years adapted to the physical changes typical of older adulthood, and developed new and fresh methods and approaches to the act of painting. Thus, in addition to imagination and inventiveness, creativity typically involves adaptability, a capacity that older adults are often thought to lack (e.g., note the frequent observation that older adults are "set in their ways").

Part 3 consists of two chapters that draw on the idea that if older adults are creative, their creativity finds expression in the very artistry of aging. Chapter 6 employs two articles by William James (one of which is "The Energies of Men") to suggest that the life of the older adult may— and often does—reflect the qualities of a relaxed body, an emancipated mind, and a spirit of dominant calm. Chapter 7 focuses on the well-attested fact that older adults tend to experience mood changes, some of which are considered by themselves and others to be rather negative. I focus especially on the view that older men become rather grumpy, and use the story of Snow White and the Seven Dwarfs[12] to suggest that their happy and grumpy dispositions can live peacefully together. (Of course, whether other persons can live peacefully with these individuals is another issue, and one that is beyond the scope of this book.)

Finally, in the epilogue I consider the possibility that young-adult readers of this book may envision a vocation in which they minister to older adults. Drawing on Henri Nouwen's pastoral image of the wounded healer,[13] I suggest that young ministers and older adults have something in common, namely, their experience of loneliness. In effect, I propose that their ministry to older adults may be informed by the fact that when they see an older adult, they experience a moment of self-recognition despite their differences in age, physical appearance, and the like.

As I noted above, the concluding chapter in part 2 includes a brief discussion of artists who in their late adulthood produced works of art that reflected new ways of viewing, understanding, and appreciating the world. The American painter Anna Mary Robertson Moses (popularly known as Grandma Moses) especially exemplifies the creative self in older adulthood because she did not begin her painting career until the age of eighty, when arthritis in her hands forced her to give up knitting. But she also exemplifies the fact that older adulthood is a period of

12. Weyn, *Snow White and the Seven Dwarfs*.

13. Nouwen, *The Wounded Healer*; also see Dykstra, ed., *Images of Pastoral Care*, 69–70, 76–84.

continuing growth and development, for in her midnineties her painting style began to change. As Jane Kallir writes in her biography of Grandma Moses,

> In part, one may be tempted to seek an explanation for the changes in Moses' late work in her attempt to control a growing unsteadiness of hand. It is apparent, however, that the artist was quite aware of what she was doing and that it was intentional. "I'm changing my style," she said in a 1956 interview, "getting modern in my old age, with a head full of ideas." The late style was not a diminishment but a triumph of her creativity.[14]

Perhaps it was no accident that her last painting, which was painted the year she died (in 1961 at the age of 101) was titled *Rainbow*, thus recalling the story of Noah and the fact that the rainbow was the sign of God's covenant with every living creature who was with Noah in the ark, and with all their future generations (Gen 9:12–16). As the rainbow was for God a reminder of the covenant, may it also be a reminder to us that God is the original Creative Self.

14. Kallir, *Grandma Moses*, 148.

PART 1

The Transition to Older Adulthood

1

Fired Up and Loaded for Bear

· · · · ·

Fire up: to animate or inspire; to excite, stimulate; to become
excited or aroused

Loaded for bear: ready and eager to deal with something that
is going to be difficult

· · · · ·

FOR THE PURPOSES OF this book, I will assume that older adulthood begins at age seventy. There are those who would argue that it begins earlier—say, at age sixty-five—but many sixty-five-year-olds do not view themselves as older adults. They accept the fact that they are transitioning into older adulthood, but they do not think that they are there yet. There are also those who are in their early seventies who do not believe that they are older adults, but I tend to believe that persuading others that they are right about this is no simple task. So I assume that for all practical purposes anyone who is seventy or older is, in fact, an older adult.

The question of how one feels about being an older adult is, of course, a whole other issue. As noted in the introduction, I found the idea of older adulthood rather discouraging. Not very many persons are elated about the fact that they have entered older adulthood, and those who are tend to have special reasons for being so, such as the fact that they did not believe that they would live to seventy, or that they have finally gained release from onerous and unfulfilling occupations. On the other hand, there are not many persons who have really strong negative feelings about becoming an older adult. Despondency or anger about the fact that one is entering older adulthood is usually thought to be a rather excessive response to a situation that everyone will face in their lives if they live to seventy. To be sure, one may have strong negative emotions because of certain circumstances that accompany entering older adulthood, such as retirement, relocation, economic challenges, physical disabilities, and so forth. But the simple fact that one has entered older adulthood does not ordinarily produce strong emotions either way. Probably the more prevalent attitude that this fact elicits is that of resignation, which the dictionary defines as "patient submission; passive acceptance; acquiescence."[1] As many older adults have been heard to say, "Well, it had to come, sooner or later," to which other older adults have responded, "I would have preferred later than sooner." To be sure, many older adults say that they are "looking forward" to their "golden years," and, no doubt, there are those who genuinely feel this way. But more often than not, their flat tone of voice when they say this seems to betray their real feelings of resignation, their passive acceptance and acquiescence, the feeling that one may as well make the best of it.

This chapter is about my own struggles with the anticipation and, subsequently, the reality of entering older adulthood. I do not present it as a model for others to follow, and I am also aware of the fact that one part of me views what I will be saying here as so much whistling in the dark. But there is another part of me that feels quite strongly about what I will be suggesting here, and as the thoughts presented here were originally expressed when I turned seventy, I can attest to the fact that I have not had any reason to think they were misguided or wrongheaded. On the contrary, I think there is a lot to be said for them. Moreover, I tend to trust the insights I have gained into myself that have come as a result of my having reflected on a poem that has, for some inexplicable reason, engaged my interest at one or another period or stage of my life. In the following discussion of the poem, I will make clear its relevance to my transition to older adulthood in the concluding paragraphs of the chapter.

1. Agnes et al., eds., *Webster's New World College Dictionary*, 1220.

Smokey the Bear and Becoming an Older Adult

The poem is Billy Collins's "Flames."[2] It was published in 1988. At the time I first read it, the possibility that it may have any personal relevance was the farthest thing from my mind. Here is the poem:

Flames

Smokey the Bear heads
into the autumn woods
with a red can of gasoline
and a box of wooden matches.

His ranger's hat is cocked
at a disturbing angle.

His brown fur gleams
under the high sun
as his paws, the size
of catchers' mitts,
crackle into the distance.

He is sick of dispensing
warnings to the careless,
the half-wit camper,
the dumbbell hiker.

He is going to show them
how a professional does it.

When I first read the poem, my heart went out to Smokey. After all, he had been devoting his life to forest-fire prevention, a most worthy cause. I could also understand how he might crack one day out of frustration and set a fire himself. After all, there is a great deal of precedence for this very reversal in the annals of *human* history: where someone who has been devoted to a worthy cause for many years throws in the towel and joins the opposition. But I found this reversal in the case of Smokey the Bear difficult to fathom, so I turned to Sigmund Freud for an explanation.

2. Collins, *The Apple That Astonished Paris*, 27.

Possible Reasons for Smokey's Behavior

Readers may wonder why I turned to Freud for an explanation for Smokey's strange behavior, but I remembered that Freud had written about how one can suppress some negative or destructive motivations and keep them hidden—even from oneself—and then suddenly give vent to them. Was this what Smokey the Bear was doing? Freud, I recalled, termed this phenomenon a *reaction-formation* and described how it works in his book *Inhibitions, Symptoms, and Anxiety.*[3] He presented this scenario: Suppose a person has an inner conflict due to ambivalent feelings toward another person. He or she has a well-grounded love for this person but a no less justifiable hatred toward this person. Freud suggested that a typical outcome of such conflicts is that one of the two conflicting feelings (usually the affectionate one) becomes greatly intensified while the other feeling completely vanishes. However, the exaggerated degree and compulsive character of the chosen feeling betray the fact that this is not the only feeling present, but that it is, in fact, constantly on the alert to keep the opposing feeling under repression.

But what if the repression fails for one reason or another and the conflicting feeling reappears? Typically, it emerges with great force— with force greater than if the feeling had been allowed to express itself more naturally in the meantime.[4] Conceivably, then, Smokey the Bear's dedication to forest-fire prevention was an exaggeration of one side of an ambivalence involving two strongly conflicting feelings: the desire to prevent forest fires and the desire to set forest fires. His given name of Smokey may have stimulated a greater fascination with forest fires than is typical of young male bears.

Another possibility, however, is that there was something deeply symbolic for Smokey about fire. In *Civilization and Its Discontents* Freud suggests that the first acts of civilization were the use of tools, the construction of buildings, and the control over fire. He adds, "Among these, the control over fire stands out as a quite extraordinary and unexampled achievement."[5] Why extraordinary? Because the stimulus behind the other acts of civilization is rather easy to guess: they have enabled humans to perfect their own organs, whether motor or sensory, or to remove the limits of their functioning. Gaining control over fire is something entirely

---

3. Freud, *Inhibitions, Symptoms, and Anxiety.*
4. Ibid., 23.
5. Freud, *Civilization and Its Discontents*, 42.

different. Freud suggests that it may be that whenever they came into contact with fire, they had the habit of satisfying an infantile desire to put the fire out by urinating on it. This, Freud believes, is a sexual act, even in young boys, because they are using their ability to urinate for pleasure, and not the mere need to eliminate urine from their bodies. I can recall when we, as young boys, referred to urinating as "putting the fire out." Freud thinks, though, that the first person who renounced this infantile desire and spared the fire was able to put the fire to his own practical use. Thus, "by damping down the fire of his own sexual excitation, he had tamed the natural force of fire."[6] Thus, instinctual renunciation led to a great cultural conquest.

Freud expands on this point in his later article "The Acquisition of Power over Fire."[7] Here, he reaffirms his idea that the acquisition of the use of fire required the renunciation of the pleasure of putting the fire out by urinating on it, and he supports this idea by focusing on the Greek myth of Prometheus. Prometheus's acquisition of fire is represented as a crime—an act of robbery or theft—and an outrage, and his punishment was to be chained to a rock, with a vulture feeding on his liver every day. Why was Prometheus punished for his so-called crime, and why with this form of punishment? Freud thinks the answer lies in the fact that the liver was selected as the physical locus on punishment. The liver, after all, "was regarded as the seat of all passions and desires," and this being so, the god of instincts (what Freud calls the Id) attacked the liver of the one who "had renounced his instinctual desires and had shown how beneficent and at the same time how essential was such renunciation for the purposes of civilization."[8] In effect, Prometheus was the target of "an instinct-ridden humanity" that resented "the demand for renunciation of instinct and its enforcement."[9]

What's interesting about Freud's reflections on fire is that he emphasizes the positive value of fire as far as human civilization is concerned. Prometheus is "the hero of civilization" because he does not indulge the instinctual desire to put the fire out in a ritual that might well be referred to as a "pissing contest." Instead, he saves the fire from extinction. Superficially, the situation that Smokey the Bear confronts is quite different,

6. Ibid., 43.

7. Freud, "The Acquisition of Power over Fire."

8. Ibid., 296.

9. Ibid., 297.

because here the issue is that fire can be terribly destructive. In fact, when a rampaging forest fire is involved, the third act of civilization (the construction of buildings for people to live and to work in) is jeopardized.

On the other hand, what appears to be a major difference between the two situations is not as significant as we might think. For, at bottom, both situations have to do with *who* acquires control over fire. In the case of Prometheus, he has taken control of fire away from those who used it for instinctual gratification, and they resent it. In the case presented in Billy Collins's poem, the half-wit camper and dumbbell hiker have acquired control of fire, and Smokey the Bear is the one who deeply resents this fact. In effect, Prometheus and Smokey are allies, as they are the heroes of civilization and are doing what they can to keep fire out of the hands of those who misuse it—either by pissing on it or by creating forest fires. What both misuses seem to have in common is the fact that fire symbolizes passions and desires inimical to the higher purposes of civilization.[10] Thus, according to this theory, Smokey's decision to set fire to the forest is a result of his profound resentment of the fact that he, one of the heroes of civilization, seems to be fighting a losing battle against the mindless proponents of instinctual gratification. They may claim that their act of setting fire to the forest was an accident, but Smokey knows better. They did it out of a desire and passion of which they themselves may not be fully aware, and he is going to show them that in their performance of these uncivilized behaviors they are rank amateurs—that they are not even good at doing what is merely instinctual and does not require much (if any) skill. In other words, if the opponents of civilization allege that Prometheus and others like him are proponents of civilization because they are inept in the realm of instinctual gratification, Smokey's idea is to show the opponents of civilization that this is not the case, and that their argument is a fallacious one.

---

10. In *The Psychology of Fire* (chapters 6, 10, and 12), the British psychiatrist Donald Scott discusses the various ways individuals abuse fire for their own illicit and violent ends. He notes that they exploit the fact that fire is untamed and uncontrolled in order to carry out aggressive acts of various kinds. In addition to those who use fire for political ends, there is the "fire-bug," who uses fire for his own disordered pleasure as well as to bring havoc on society; and the psychotic person, who uses fire to take revenge against someone who has insulted him, either in reality or fantasy.

Irony: The Art of Saying the Opposite
of What You Really Mean

A third way of reading the poem with psychoanalytic eyes is to consider Freud's discussion of irony in *Jokes and Their Relation to the Unconscious*. This discussion appears in his chapter on the techniques of jokes.[11] One of these techniques is to say the opposite of what is really meant or intended. For example, Freud relates a joke about a beggar who had come to the baron's palace in hopes of receiving a gift of charity. When the beggar finishes his tale of woe to the baron, the baron rings for his servants. When they arrive, he says to them, "Throw this man out! He's breaking my heart."[12] The baron suggests that the beggar's story is so heartbreaking that he cannot handle it emotionally. We know, though, that this is simply a way to justify the act of dismissing the beggar without giving him anything at all.

Here's a more contemporary example of the joke technique of saying the opposite of what is meant:

> A minister, a priest, and a rabbi were playing poker when the police raided the game. Turning to the minister, the lead police officer said, "Reverend Allsworth, were you gambling?" Turning his eyes to heaven the minister whispered, "Lord, forgive me for what I am about to do." To the police officer he said, "No, officer, I was not gambling." The officer then asked the priest, "Father Murphy, were you gambling?" Again, after an appeal to heaven, the priest replied, "No, officer, I was not gambling." Turning to the rabbi, the officer again asked, "Rabbi Goldman, were you gambling?" Shrugging his shoulders, the rabbi replied, "With whom?"[13]

In this joke the minister and the priest simply tell a lie—they say no when the truthful answer would have been yes. If the rabbi had responded in the same way, there would be no joke. The joke is in the fact that he neither lies nor tells the truth, but says, in effect, "If these two fellows weren't gambling, I could not have been gambling either, because in poker it requires two or more to gamble."

Freud notes that the technique of "representation by its opposite" is by no means unique to jokes, and adds that it is frequently used in

11. Freud, *Jokes and Their Relation to the Unconscious*, 86.
12. Ibid., 135.
13. Tapper and Press, *A Minister, a Priest, and a Rabbi*, 172.

irony. He cites the case of a well-known Munich weekly comic magazine that describes a collection of incredible instances of brutality as the expressions of "men of feeling," and he suggests that whereas jokes make use of various techniques, "the only technique that characterizes irony is representation by the opposite."[14]

Because Freud is concerned in this chapter with joke techniques, he does not discuss irony any further. Later, though, he returns to irony in his chapter on the relation of jokes to dreams and to the unconscious mind. In a discussion of the fact that dreams and jokes use similar techniques, one of which is representation by its opposite, he mentions his earlier reference to irony and suggests that "it comes very close to joking," and adds, "Its essence lies in saying the opposite of what one intends to convey to the other person, but in sparing him contradiction by making him understand—by one's tone of voice, by some accompanying gesture, or (where writing is concerned) by some small stylistic indications—that one means the opposite of what one says."[15]

Rabbi Goldman's shrug of his shoulders is an example of such an accompanying gesture. Freud notes, however, that irony is subject to being misunderstood. Thinking that the speaker means what he or she says, the hearer feels compelled to contradict it. If, however, the hearer understands that the speaker is saying the opposite of what he or she actually means, then the pleasure of the irony lies in the fact that the hearer's "contradictory expenditure of energy" is recognized as unnecessary. In other words, the pleasure we gain from irony is that we save in the expenditure of our own mental energy. We don't have to marshal an argument against the speaker at all.[16]

The idea that the essence of irony lies in the fact that one says the opposite of what one intends to convey to the other person applies especially well to the poet who, in this case, is Billy Collins. We would misunderstand the poem if we thought that he is suggesting that Smokey the Bear *should* set fire to the forest with his can of gasoline and boxful of matches in order to show the camper and hiker how to do a really professional job of burning the forest down. We know that Collins is not suggesting this at all, and because we know this, we do not feel compelled to contradict him: "Look here, Mr. Collins, a real professional like Smokey

14. Freud, *Jokes and Their Relation to the Unconscious*, 86.
15. Ibid., 215–16.
16. Ibid., 216. The savings in this case is likely to be a savings in *difficult thinking*.

the Bear would not show these careless and stupid people how to burn the forest down; on the contrary, he would try to show them how *not* to set fire to the forest."

If we *were* to raise this objection, Mr. Collins might feel constrained to point out the obvious: "I'm not actually suggesting that Smokey the Bear should set fire to the forest. I'm making the point that Smokey has been devoting his life to controlling forest fires by teaching everyone some basic rules for how to avoid setting fires. Yet the dumbbells and half-wits still cause forest fires. Noting this fact is what the poem is basically about." We know, of course, that you can ruin a good poem (or a joke) by explaining it, so it is unlikely that Mr. Collins would feel constrained to point out the obvious. More likely, he would simply shrug his shoulders and follow Smokey into the woods to witness the conflagration.

The Moral of the Story

I think that all three of these interpretations of the poem are plausible, but they focus on different things. The first interpretation—reaction formation—focuses on Smokey's unconscious mind, and posits that his dedication of his life to prevention of forest fires suggests a repressed desire to set forests ablaze. The second interpretation—that the desire to acquire control over fire reflects a civilizing intention that requires the renunciation of instinctual gratification—focuses on Smokey's cultural role as a hero of civilization. These two interpretations are not, of course, incompatible, because Smokey's dedication of his life to the prevention of forest fires is congruent with the cultural role of the hero of civilization. Also, although they offer different explanations for what he is about to do (ambivalence of feeling in the first case and desire for instinctual gratification in the second), they both assume that Smokey has been repressing certain feelings or desires that he can repress no longer, and that he is now prepared to sacrifice his position and stature as a hero of civilization as the price he is willing to pay for the relief and the pleasure of giving vent to these feelings and desires.

If the first two interpretations, then, focus on what is going on in Smokey's psyche, the third is more concerned with what's going on in the poem (i.e., with the poem's *technique*). Freud helps us to see that *irony* is what's going on in the poem, and this means that it is saying the opposite of what it means. This, in turn, means that the poet is attempting to

convey a truth about people who cause forest fires, however unintentionally, which is that these people tend to disprove the claim that we humans
are the most intelligent of all the animal species. Collins makes this point
by suggesting that a bear is about to teach them a lesson in setting forest
fires. As Wayne C. Booth points out, irony can end in nihilism, but this
need not be the case and often is not the case, for irony is often employed
in order to express a conviction that might otherwise be ignored or disre-
garded.[17] The concluding lines of the poem—"He is going to show them
how a professional does it"—says, in effect, that as forest-fire setters go,
these guys are really lousy at it. If you are going to set a forest fire, you
might at least make a professional job of it.

I believe that all three interpretations are useful and pertinent to
the poem, but the third one is more interesting to me because it enables
me to read the poem as one that has relevance to a much wider range
of human concerns than that of forest-fire prevention, important as this
concern is. The key to the poem's broader applicability is the fact that
the final couplet—"He is going to show them / how a professional does
it"—is profoundly ironic. Smokey's claim to be a professional is based on
the fact that he has become a professional, as it were, from watching how
the amateurs tend to botch the job, and not from any desire to become
good at it himself.

As I thought about the poem's irony, it occurred to me that this irony had relevance to my own life-situation: I was on the verge of entering
older adulthood, and like most persons who enter older adulthood, and
I had been rather unhappy about the prospect of entering the autumn
of my life. (Note that the poem is set in autumn.) I was also aware of
the fact that the vast majority of older adults would prefer to be younger
adults. As Sharon Kaufman, author of *The Ageless Self,* discovered in her
interviews with older adults, most of us like to think of ourselves as being much younger than we actually are. Most of Kaufman's interviewees
thought of themselves as pretty much the person they were when they
were many years younger.[18] When they say that they feel they are essentially the same person they were at thirty or forty-five, they immediately
observe that, of course, they look much older, but this fact has little, if
anything, to do with who they feel themselves to be inside. A seventy-
year-old woman said that she feels like she's the same person she was at

17. Booth, *A Rhetoric of Irony,* 244.
18. Kaufman, *The Ageless Self,* 8–12.

age thirty, and another woman, who was eighty-four years old, showed Kaufman a photo of herself taken when she was twenty-nine, and when Kaufman asked her if she "related" to the woman in the photo she replied, "I feel the same now as I did then, oh yes."[19] This makes a lot of sense to me, as I think this is pretty much the age with which I tend to identify my inner self.

On the other hand, this very identification with one's younger self may reveal a deeper truth, namely, that one is resisting the very idea that one is, in fact, an older adult. If we in our adolescent years had resisted the fact that we were in fact adolescents and not children anymore, the adults in our lives would undoubtedly have counseled us to accept the fact that we were adolescents. The same holds true, I believe, for older adults. Better to embrace the fact that we are older adults than to resist it. In fact, if the irony of Collins's poem is that Smokey is going to show those who are rather indifferent, amateurish fire-setters how a real professional goes about it, would not this irony also apply to entering older adulthood? Rather than entering it reluctantly or halfheartedly, why not demonstrate to ourselves—and perhaps to others—how a real professional performs older adulthood? In other words, why not make a virtue out of a constitutional necessity?[20] I cannot speak for Collins, the writer of the poem, but I can speak for myself as a reader for whom the poem is truly inspiring: "Smokey, lead the way. I'll carry the red can of gasoline. You bring the box of matches."

19. Ibid., 12. In *Early Bird: A Memoir of Premature Retirement*, Rodney Rothman relates his experience of living for several months in a retirement community in Boca Raton, Florida. He had lost his job because the television show he was working on was cancelled. Given that his first vacations in his boyhood had been spent in Florida visiting his grandparents, he decided to move to Florida temporarily and, in effect, retire early. He was twenty-eight years old at the time, or roughly the age that the older adults in Kaufman's study identified with. It turned out that Rodney adapted so well to living with older adults that he was reluctant to leave when his agent secured another job for him.

20. Erikson, *Childhood and Society* (1st ed.), 13.

2

A Faithful Reunion

· · · · ·

Reunion: the act of reuniting; a gathering of persons after separation

Faithful: steadfast, reliable, conscientious

Mentor: a wise, loyal adviser; a teacher or coach

· · · · ·

THE PRECEDING CHAPTER ENDED on a rather self-assured—some might say pretentious—note. I would set aside my resistances to entering older adulthood and instead go charging into it with confidence and passion, and show the timorous ones how a professional does it. In most fields of endeavor, it takes years of concentrated effort and self-discipline to become a professional. Yet I was going to show everyone, including those who had been planning for their entry into older adulthood, how a real professional does it. The very idea that I would do this in spite of the fact that I hadn't given it any more thought than had the half-wit camper and dumbbell hiker given prior thought to how to create a forest fire seems rather ridiculous.

Clearly, I would need help in making the transition to older adult-hood, and several colleagues and friends pointed out to me the various avenues for obtaining help. These included asking people who *were* professionals to tell me their secrets, reading books on the subject, and going to talks and lectures sponsored by retirement communities near where I live. I did the first two but could not bring myself to do the third. These conversations and books were most helpful, but this chapter is about a resource that I drew upon that no one had talked to me about, and that I stumbled upon by chance. This chapter is not so much an argument for this particular resource—although I would certainly recommend it—as it is a case for developing one's own approach or method. In fact, the resource that I drew upon stood in marked contrast to the approaches that I have mentioned, all of which tend to involve listening to expert advisers. The process began with the announcement of the reunion marking the fiftieth anniversary of the graduation of my high school class.

My High School Reunion

A few years ago I received a mailing advising that I mark my calendar for a very important event: my high school class's fiftieth-year reunion party was approaching. The date had been set, and it was time to make reservations. A list of class members who were known to have died and another list of classmates whose whereabouts were unknown were included in the mailing. We were asked to supply any information we might have about the unknown so that they too could be sent a copy of the mailing.

As I read through the list of those who had died, I had a sickening feeling not unlike the feeling that many have when they visit the Vietnam War Memorial in Washington DC. I was surprised that so many of the members of the class were no longer living. Then I read through the names of those who could not be located, and I had another reaction: my best friend was on that list.

I recalled that the last time I saw him was at our graduation ceremony. Neither of us made an effort to stay in touch after that. Despite the fact that his grades were excellent, he had decided not to go to college, and would not be persuaded otherwise, while I was going to take courses at the local state college in the summer so that I could begin piling up credits in hopes of getting college over with as quickly as possible. I had no time for high school friends, or, for that matter, for reflecting on my high school experience.

Now, fifty years later, I was not at all interested in attending the class reunion. I sent the class-reunion committee a check to help defray the costs of the mailings, and suggested to the committee treasurer that if the check didn't bounce, she would know that I was better off now than I had been in high school. A donation, a little joke—and I felt I was off the hook.

But the mailings kept coming: there was more information about the dress code at the country club where the dinner and dance were to be held, the fact that a tour of the high school had been arranged, and more requests for information about those whose whereabouts were unknown. My best friend had not been located. In fact, the list was essentially the same as the previous list had been. No one seemed to know the whereabouts of the missing, or if they knew, they had not taken the trouble to inform the reunion committee.

The mailings—there were several more—began to weigh on me. I'd received college-reunion mailings before, but these were summarily tossed into the wastebasket without much thought. So too were reunion mailings from the schools where I had received advanced degrees. Why did I take the time to read the high-school class-reunion mailings? Why did it concern me that my best friend had not been located? After all, would I have contacted him if he had been found? I doubt it. So what was so special or unique about these class-reunion mailings?

A couple of explanations occurred to me: One was that my retirement was imminent, and the reunion mailings took me back in time to when my initial struggles to discover my vocation in life had begun. The other was that, having announced my retirement a couple years ahead of time, I was experiencing some of the same emotions that I had first experienced as a high school student: marginalization, isolation, directionlessness, and uncertainty of what the future held for me. In other words, the mailings were as much related to the present as they were to the past.

Still, I found it rather incredible that a large number of my high school classmates would soon be gathering together to have dinner, to dance to the music of "our era," and to tour the building where we had sat in classes, eaten lunch, gone to assemblies, and made fools of ourselves in the gymnasium, either trying to learn modern dance steps or to throw a ball into a ten-foot-high basket. Why would they want to relive those memories? Why would they risk meeting someone with whom they thought they were in love but who dumped them for someone else? Why would they chance seeing the guy who beat them out for a starting position on the varsity baseball team while they sat on the bench, game after game, trying their best to put the good of the team ahead of their own personal ambition and profound disappointment? Why would some of them risk the likelihood that no one would remember who they were, or of finding themselves without anyone to talk with?

I posed these questions to a friend who had recently attended his own fiftieth-year high school reunion party. Why did he go? Well, he had grown up in a working-class part of town, and he wanted his high school classmates to know that he had made good in his professional life. But, more important, the reunion committee had mentioned in one of their mailings that several of their teachers had agreed to attend the reunion dinner, and one of these teachers was a man who had inspired him to set his personal and vocational goals far beyond his working-class status.

"Did you have a good time?" I asked.

"Yes, I was able to impress a lot of people with what I did in life. On the other hand, I got into an argument with this one jerk because he wouldn't move to another table so that the teacher who meant so much to me could sit in a place of honor. He was a jerk then, and he's still a jerk."

This was not a very persuasive explanation for why someone would go to a high school reunion. But the very fact that it was not persuasive forced me to ask myself why I found the mailings not only irritating but also unexpectedly troubling, and the fact that my best friend could not be located provided a useful clue to why this was so: as the mailings kept coming, I slowly realized that the class reunion was not, after all, the issue. Rather, the real issue was that the high school boy who was somewhere deep inside me was missing too. When I left high school with such finality and determination to get on with my life, I had left him behind—wandering about the empty halls, lost, as it were, in a kind of modern limbo not unlike the medieval version where, as Dante suggests, the lamentations of its occupants "are not the shrieks of pain, but hopeless sighs."[1]

Then, however, it occurred to me that he might not be the lamentable one, for I reminded myself of the fact that many artists have portrayed Christ's descent into limbo and, in doing so, infused its occupants with a profound sense of hope.[2] This being so, perhaps my need to find him was greater than his need to find me.

---

1. Quoted in Le Goff, *The Birth of Purgatory,* 336.
2. See Capps and Carlin, *Living in Limbo,* 7–8.

But how should I go about finding him? Photos were somewhat helpful. Recollections stored in my mind were also useful. But, in the end, I decided to consider what he wrote during his senior year in high school, specifically, a story that was written for a creative writing class and published in a national student magazine.[3]

In the following exploration, I will view this story from the perspective of the older man who, years later, has found it (and several other high school writings) an invaluable means to experience a reunion with his younger self, and I will relate how this younger self became my mentor in my transition to older adulthood via the story he had written. I had not read the story (of which I had a copy) in many years, and I had not known of the existence of the other writings until after my father's death in 1990 led to the sale of the family home and distribution of its contents to my brothers and me. Even then, I gave them little attention until the high school class-reunion mailings continued to appear in my mailbox.

The Story of Olav and Charlie

The story, titled "Charlie," is set in western Nebraska. Some years before I wrote it, our family had visited the Lutheran mission in Axtell, where my cousin Christine had lived since birth; my uncle and aunt had been advised that it was best to place Down syndrome children in an institution. I recall that my uncle was so distressed when he broke the news to my parents that his newborn daughter was "a Mongoloid" (the term used at the time for children with Down syndrome) that I, four or five years old at the time, asked my mother if my cousin had died.[4]

While my parents visited with Christine and members of the staff, my brothers and I remained outside the building. We were entertained by a male resident who seemed to have some sort of mental abnormality. He asked us if we were from Funk, a nearby town, and when my father appeared, the man patted my father's paunch and said, "I'll go get my ball too." His Funk query and his association of our father's paunch with a ball amused us so much that we often repeated the query—"You from

3. Capps, "Charlie."

4. In a scrapbook I compiled in 1948 (when I was nine years old) there is a typed list of 37 dates to remember, most relating to the births of United States presidents. But two entries stand out—one indicates that National Child Health Day is May 1, the other notes that the first orphanage in the United States opened on August 7, 1727.

Funk?"—when we happened to encounter one another, and we too would pat our father's stomach and say, "I'll go get my ball too."

This man became the main character in my story. I called him Charlie and represented him as a former farmer who was a resident in the mission, but who left every morning to hang around in the town and then returned to the mission later in the day. I suggested that he was frequently engaged in conversation with the boys in town, who enjoyed teasing him mildly, to which he would respond good-naturedly.

But this particular morning, he was in no mood for light banter. During the night, a young boy named Olav (a variant form of Olaf, a popular Scandinavian name) had found his way out of the mission building without anyone noticing and had disappeared. A rescue party had been formed, and when it failed to find him in town, it concentrated its efforts on the prairie beyond the town. Charlie told the boys that morning that he was worried about Olav: "He ain't too strong, especially that game leg. Someone's got to do something." The boys didn't share his anguish: "Why don't you do it? We gotta go catch rabbits. It's been nice talkin' with you." After they hurried off, Charlie continued talking to himself, mainly about needing a new milkweed to put into his mouth, then told himself that he would never be able to find Olav "jest talkin' here to myself," and he began walking.

Meanwhile, the mission chapel was filled with vigil keepers, many of whom expressed disbelief that Olav could have gone. Maybe he was only hiding, playing a trick as he had done so many times. Did someone search the barn where the old tomcat stays? Yes, "but he wasn't there." Then the boys returned from chasing rabbits and found that Charlie was gone. "Hey, where's crazy Charlie?" No one seemed to know. They asked Jake, a kid who was hanging around, if he knew anything about what had happened to Charlie. He replied, "Don't know. My dad says he took off mumbling that he thought Olav had something he had to find and that he thought he could help Olav find it."

The story shifts at this point to Charlie and his search for Olav. It relates that

> Charlie walked on, through cornfields, over fences, and waded through streams and the Papio Creek, until he at last came to the bluff overlooking the mission. He turned, gazing back. They'll miss me at the mission, he thought. "Maybe I oughta go back."

Instead, he decided to keep going: "No, Olav went exploring, and he'll find it. He knows, he's headed somewhere special."

At this point the narrator comments on the terrain, "One doesn't know how long a mile can be until he's walked a Nebraska mile, a sandy, dusty, choking mile," and says of Charlie,

> Cockleburs clung to his ankles and stung. The brush cut deeply into his leg, and he slowed down. He picked up a handful of sand and let it fall from his fingers. The prairie, rolling, rolling. A weary old man trudging, with a faraway look in his sun-squinted eyes—a look which seemed to pierce through things, deeply, compassionately. A crazy old man on a foolish trek, tired, almost to the point of giving in. He stumbled once and slowly raised himself. He looked over his shoulder and cried, "I won't be back!" It echoed through the cornfields until it whispered through the mission gate, "I won't be back." Charlie's gone. He went to find the boy, Olav. He won't be back. He won't be back. And on he trudged. And the sand sifted slowly through his clutching hand, the sun settled silently on the treeless bluff, and a weary man stumbled and fell to the ground with that faraway look in his tear-glistened eyes. "Olav, I've found you! Don't wait for me. I'm catching up, Olav, my boy, I've found you." The sun sank slowly on the quiet bluff, and the sand no longer sifted through his clutching hand.

With this, the story ends.

I am not concerned here with evaluating the story as a piece of creative writing. Instead, my interest lies in what the story tells me about the high school boy who wrote it. With this in mind, I would especially take note of the narrator's emphasis on the fact that the boy did not wander off the mission grounds for no good reason. Rather, there was a purpose to his decision to leave the mission. He was embarking on a quest, headed, as Charlie perceived, "somewhere special." Also, because the mission was all that he had ever known, this "somewhere special" was not the home where he had lived prior to becoming a resident at the mission. This "somewhere special" serves as an image of hope.[5] This image is intentionally undefined. The narrator does not say, for example, that the boy's quest was for heaven, or that he was drawn by the magnetism of God. As the reader, I am rather pleased that the narrator left the object of the boy's quest indistinct, because an effort to identify it more precisely

---

5. See Lynch, *Images of Hope.* See also Capps, *Agents of Hope,* 64–71.

would have turned the story into an overtly religious story. There were already enough religious associations in the story with its references to the mission and, more specifically, the mission chapel where the vigil keepers had gathered.

A second observation concerns the relationship of the old man and the young boy. The story reverses the usual expectation that the older man is the one who leads and the young boy is the one who follows. Not here. The old man is drawn by the power of the boy who is in quest of "something special." But, as the story comes to a close, the old man does not say that he too wants what the boy is searching for. Instead, he declares, "Olav, I've found you! Don't wait for me. I'm catching up. Olav, my boy, I've found you." His search is for the boy himself. But Charlie doesn't want the boy to wait for him. Instead, he wants Olav to keep going, and he will do the catching up. As he lies on the ground, Charlie declares that he has, in fact, found the boy.

As I view the story from my own vantage point as an older man, I have a deep sense of being Charlie and of my younger self as Olav. An older man is tempted to view his younger self as struggling to discover what the older man, through time and effort, has managed to find for himself. But Charlie is far wiser than this. He understands that it is the boy who is out ahead, searching for what he knows, and that he, the older man, is the one who is trying to catch up. We might say that the older self has the benefit of hindsight, but the younger self has the benefit of foresight. And as Erik H. Erikson points out in *Toys and Reasons* in his chapter titled "Seeing Is Hoping," a play on the familiar saying that "seeing is believing," *vision* has two meanings, namely, "the capacity to see what is before us, here and now, and the power to foresee what, if one can only believe it, might yet prove true in the future."[6]

The Mentor Relationship

As I have reflected on this story and the other writings from my high school days, I have come to think of this boy—my younger self—as my mentor. A brief discussion of Daniel J. Levinson's section on "The Mentor Relationship" in *The Seasons of a Man's Life* will help to explain what I mean when I make this claim.[7] Levinson's book is based on his and

6. Erikson, *Toys and Reasons*, 46.

7. Levinson, *The Seasons of a Man's Life*, 97–101. While this book was written by

his colleagues' study of forty men who were between the ages of thirty-five and forty-five when the research study got underway. Levinson felt intuitively that the years around age forty have a special importance in a person's life, and that these years represent the shift from young adulthood to middle adulthood. In the interviews, the men were encouraged to talk about their lives in earlier years, with particular emphasis on their adult years (twenties and thirties). In the course of these interviews, one of the features of what Levinson calls "the novice phase" (from roughly seventeen to thirty-two years of age) is the mentor relationship. It is one of the four major tasks of the novice phase. The others are forming and living out the Dream, forming an occupation, and forming a marriage and family.[8]

In his discussion of the mentor relationship, Levinson states that this relationship "is one of the most complex, and developmentally important, a man can have in early adulthood."[9] He goes on to note that the mentor "is ordinarily several years older, a person of greater experience and seniority in the world the young man is entering." He adds:

> No word currently in use is adequate to convey the nature of the relationship we have in mind here. Words such as "counselor" or "guru" suggest the more subtle meanings, but they have other connotations that would be misleading. The term "mentor" is generally used in a much narrower sense, to mean teacher, adviser, or sponsor. As we use the term, it means all of these things, and more.[10]

The mentor relationship is often located in a work setting, and the mentoring functions are often assumed by a teacher, boss, or senior colleague. But it may evolve informally when the mentor is an older friend, neighbor, or relative. It is not defined in terms of formal roles but by the

---

Levinson, the title page indicates that he had the collaboration of four others (Charlotte N. Darrow, Edward B. Klein, Maria J. Levinson, and Braxton McKee), all of whom were members of his research team at Yale University. His second book, *The Seasons of a Woman's Life,* was written with the collaboration of Judy D. Levinson, who arranged for its posthumous publication.

8. Levinson, *The Seasons of a Man's Life,* 90–111.

9. Ibid., 97.

10. Ibid., 97. Agnes et al., eds., *Webster's New World College Dictionary* notes that in Greek mythology Mentor was the loyal friend and adviser of Odysseus and teacher of his son Telemachus. Definitions of *mentor* are "a wise, loyal adviser" and "a teacher or coach" (900).

character of the relationship and the functions it serves. These are the major functions of the mentor:

> He may act as a *teacher* to enhance the young man's skills and intellectual development. Serving as *sponsor,* he may use his influence to facilitate the young man's entry and advancement. He may be a *host* and *guide,* welcoming the initiate into a new occupational and social world and acquainting him with its values, customs, resources, and cast of characters. Through his own virtues, the mentor may be an exemplar that the protégé can admire and seek to emulate. He may provide counsel and moral support in time of stress.[11]

In addition to these functions, the mentor may have another function—one that, in Levinson's view, is developmentally the most crucial. This is the support and facilitation of the younger man's realization of his Dream. In its primordial form, the Dream is a vague sense of self-in-adult world. It has the quality of a vision, an imagined possibility that generates excitement and vitality. Initially, it is poorly articulated and only tenuously connected to reality, but as time goes on, the developmental task is to give it greater definition and to find ways to live it out.[12] This is where the mentor can be of great importance as he "fosters the young adult's development by believing in him, sharing his youthful Dream and giving it his blessing, helping to define the newly emerging self in its newly discovered world, and creating a space in which the young man can work on a reasonably satisfactory life structure that contains the Dream."[13]

Levinson emphasizes that the mentor's primary function is to be a transitional figure, and this means that he cannot be the young man's father (or mother).[14] In early adulthood a young man needs to shift from being a child in relation to parental adults to being an adult in a peer relationship with other adults. This means that the mentor represents a

---

11. Levinson, *The Seasons of a Man's Life,* 98. Levinson refers to the mentor in the male gender because this reflected the fact that all the men in the study had had male mentors. He adds, however, that "a mentor may be either the same gender or cross gender" and a "relationship with a female mentor can be an enormously valuable experience for a young man, as I know from personal experience" (98).

12. Ibid., 91.

13. Ibid., 99.

14. Levinson is implicitly drawing here on D. W. Winnicott's concept of the "transitional object" as presented in his article "Transitional Objects and Transitional Phenomena," originally published in 1953 and republished in his *Playing and Reality,* 1–25.

mixture of parent and peer and cannot be entirely one or the other: "If he is entirely a peer, he cannot represent the advanced level toward which the younger man is striving," and "if he is very parental, it is difficult for both of them to overcome the generational difference and move toward the peer relationship that is the ultimate (though never fully realized) goal of the relationship."[15] Normally, the mentor who serves these transitional functions is older than his protégé by a half-generation, roughly eight to fifteen years. It is possible that one can function as a mentor even if one is twenty or even fifty years older if he is in touch with his own and the other's youthful Dreams. Conversely, a person who is the same age or even younger may have important mentoring qualities if he has unusual expertise and understanding, and if both have the maturity to make good use of the mentor's virtues. But, generally speaking, the mentor is a half-generation older than the one who is mentored.

The mentor relationship itself changes over time as the young man who is being mentored gains a fuller sense of his own authority and his capability for autonomous, responsible action. As Levinson puts it, "The younger man increasingly has the experience of 'I am' as an adult, and their relationship becomes more mutual."[16] This very shift plays a crucial role in the development of the younger man, as it signifies that the younger man has entered the adult world and is no longer a boy in a man's world.

Levinson notes that in his discussion of the mentor relationship he has described it in its most developed and constructive form, but the reality may be very different. Mentoring, he observes, is not a simple, all-or-nothing matter: "A relationship may be remarkably beneficial to the younger person and yet be seriously flawed. For example, a teacher or boss cares for and sponsors a protégé, but is so afraid of being eclipsed that he behaves destructively at crucial moments."[17] On the other hand, a relationship may be very limited and yet have great value in certain respects. For example,

> Some men have a purely symbolic mentor whom they never meet. Thus, an aspiring young novelist may admire an older

15. Ibid., 99.

16. Ibid. D. W. Winnicott uses the term "I AM" in his essay "The Value of Depression," in *Home is Where We Start From*, 71–89. Also, Erik H. Erikson discusses the individual's sense of *I* in *Identity, Youth, and Crisis*, 216–21. I will refer to Erikson's discussion later in this chapter.

17. Levinson, *The Seasons of a Man's Life*, 100.

writer, devour his books, learn a great deal about his life, and create an idealized internal figure with whom he has a complex relationship.[18]

Also, although Levinson does not make this point, the creation of an idealized internal figure is typically a feature of all mentor relationships, including those in which the two are in regular physical contact with one another.

Levinson concludes his discussion of the mentor relationship with the observation that where the relationship is "good enough,"[19] the young man feels admiration, respect, appreciation, gratitude, and love for the mentor, and these feelings outweigh but cannot entirely prevent the opposite feelings of resentment, inferiority, envy, and intimidation:

> There is a resonance between them. The elder has qualities of character, expertise and understanding that the younger admires and wants to make parts of himself. The young man is excited and spurred on by the shared sense of his promise. Yet he is also full of self-doubt. Can he ever become all that both of them want him to be? At different times—or even at the same moment—he experiences himself as the inept novice, the fraudulent imposter, the equal colleague and the rising star who will someday soar to heights far beyond those of the mentor.[20]

Also, as a transitional relationship, it is destined to terminate, usually in two or three years on the average and eight to ten years at most. It may end when one of them moves, changes jobs, or dies. Sometimes it comes to a natural end and, after a cooling-off period, develops into a warm but modest friendship. In other cases, it ends totally, with a gradual loss of involvement. Most often, though, an intense mentor relationship ends with strong conflict and bad feelings on both sides:

> The young man may have powerful feelings of bitterness, rancor, grief, abandonment, liberation and rejuvenation. The sense of resonance is lost. The mentor he formerly loved and admired is now experienced as destructively critical and demanding, or as seeking to make one over in his own image rather than fostering one's individuality and independence. The mentor who only

18. Ibid.

19. His use of the term "good-enough" to characterize the mentor relationship is derived from D. W. Winnicott's concept of the "good-enough mother" as presented in "Transitional Objects and Transitional Phenomena."

20. Levinson, *The Seasons of a Man's Life*, 100.

yesterday was regarded as an enabling teacher and friend has become a tyrannical father or smothering mother. The mentor, for his part, finds the young man inexplicably touchy, unreceptive to even the best counsel, irrationally rebellious and ungrateful. By the time they are through, there is generally some validity in each one's criticism of the other. And so it ends.[21]

And yet, Levinson notes that much of its value may be realized after the termination. The conclusion of the relationship itself does not put an end to the *meaning* of the relationship: "Following the separation, the younger man may take the admired qualities of the mentor more fully into himself," and, conversely, "He may become better able to learn from himself, to listen to the voices from within," and "His personality is enriched as he makes the mentor a more intrinsic part of himself."[22]

The Younger Self as Mentor in the Transition to Older Adulthood

In light of the foregoing presentation of Levinson's understanding of the mentor relationship, I realize that it seems rather odd to suggest that my younger self has served as my mentor in my entrance into and continuing experience of older adulthood. After all, an important characteristic of the mentor is that he is typically eight to fifteen years *older* than the young man who is the recipient of his mentoring. And even if we note Levinson's observation that the mentor may possibly be younger than the person who is being mentored, he makes it clear that this is quite rare, and, furthermore, it is very unlikely that this younger person would be able to perform all the functions of the mentor.

On the other hand, there is a sense in which one's younger self is older than one's contemporary self because this younger self represents an *earlier* stage in one's life. Thus, while my younger self is, in this instance, a high school student who is about to embark on the journey from boyhood to adulthood, he is older in the sense that he represents an earlier era and expresses convictions that I, the older man, have found invaluable in my own journey from middle to older adulthood. From *his* perspective, the fact that the older man in the story, Charlie, believes in the boy Olav and in his capacity to realize his goal in life is self-affirming.

21. Ibid., 100–101.
22. Ibid., 101.

Thus, in a sense, Charlie plays the mentor role to Olav—and to the story's author—because he believes in the young boy and in his sense of direction in life. From *my* perspective, as the older man reading the story, the fact that the young author presents the older man as having found the young boy who knows where he is going is also self-affirming, for this means that I will find my way as I embark upon and continue on the path of older adulthood.

As Levinson points out, the mentor's primary function is to be a transitional figure, one who helps his protégé make his own transition from boyhood to adulthood. The very fact that the story of Olav and Charlie is about a journey from the place they know—perhaps all too well—to a place that they envision makes it a story of transitions, both for the young man and for the older man as well. Levinson also points out that the mentor relationship can be a symbolic one, as when an aspiring young novelist devours an established author's books, learns a great deal about this author's life, and creates an idealized internal figure with which he has a complex relationship. I rediscovered the younger self, who became my mentor during my own transition to older adulthood through a story that he had written. Others have found their younger self through diaries that they wrote when they were in their teenage years. For me, however, the fact that my reunion with my younger self occurred through the agency of a fictional story was significant. I believe—and tend to think that he would concur—that we would have found a more direct reunion—one more overtly autobiographical—a rather awkward encounter and one less likely to result in the creation of an idealized internal figure. This has and will enable us to maintain the relationship as time goes on, as neither of us feels any pressure—external or internal—to terminate our relationship and go our separate ways.

The Will to Believe and Looking Forward to Tomorrow

In the box containing a scrapbook, my high school writings, and other items that were among the miscellany in my father's home, there was a poem that I wrote when I was in fourth grade—thus, at nine or ten years old. This is the poem:

Winter

Winter is a joyful season.
It is joyful—there's a reason.
Ice and snow and outdoor fun
Cozy nights when play is done.
Each day more fun than all the rest.
I know—for this day is the best.
But Mother now has called us in.
I wish tomorrow would begin.

In this much younger boy's poetic world, we have the rather unanticipated affirmation of winter as a joyful season, one filled with days of outdoor fun. This fun is interrupted by Mother's call to come in, presumably for the evening meal, but the speaker does not complain or intimate that he tarries. For, after all, he anticipates a cozy night when play is done.

It would be easy for me, the older man, to say that he is in for a rude awakening, that there will come a day when the anticipated tomorrow is worse—much worse—than today, which is already bad enough. But why should I assume that he is utterly naïve when, more than likely, he is simply a boy with an irrepressible will to believe?[23] In this regard, it may well be that he is the older boy's mentor, the sponsor, as it were, of the older boy's tendency to communicate a similar will to believe as exemplified in the story of Olav and Charlie.

This suggestion has bearing on Levinson's reference to the younger man's increasing experience of a sense of "I am" as the mentor relationship changes over time, and as the younger man gains a fuller sense of his own authority and his capability for autonomous, responsible action.[24] In his chapter titled "Theoretical Interlude" in *Identity: Youth, and Crisis*, Erik Erikson seeks to clarify what we mean when we refer to ourselves as "I." In the course of this discussion, he suggests that the *I* is composed of various selves that make up our "composite Self."[25] Erikson goes on to note the constant and often shock-like transitions between these selves, and invites us to consider the nude body self in the dark or suddenly exposed to light, the clothed self among friends or in the company of

---

23. See James, "The Will to Believe."
24. Levinson, *The Seasons of a Man's Life*, 99.
25. Erikson, *Identity, Youth, and Crisis*, 217.

higher-ups or lower-downs, and the just-awakened drowsy self or the one stepping refreshed out of the surf.[26]

I suggest that we might also view the *I* as composed of selves that emerge in the successive decades of our lives, and in my book *The Decades of Life* I draw on Erikson's own schedule of virtues (which will be discussed in chapter 3) to identify the selves of the first and second decade. These are *the hopeful self* and *the willing self*.[27] I believe that *the hopeful self* is evident in the poem on winter, and *the willing self* is evident in the story of Charlie and Olav. Also, this *willing self* is an extension, as it were, of *the hopeful self*. This means that the *I* draws on these earlier selves to facilitate the transition to older adulthood. And, as I have suggested, what these two earlier stages especially offer in this regard is the will to believe.

A central feature of this will to believe is, as Levinson notes, a belief in oneself. But Erikson also suggests that the selves that compose the sense of *I* interact with others, an interaction that, as we have seen, occurs, for example, in the mentor relationship. In fact, the mentor relationship illustrates the fact that the interaction between the *I* and other *I*'s involves a mutuality of belief—a belief in one another. This fact is implicit as well in Erikson's suggestion that the individual's sense of *I* is ultimately confirmed by God, who, when Moses asked him who should he say had called him, answered, "I AM THAT I AM," and then ordered Moses to tell the multitude, "I AM has sent me unto you" (Exod 3:13–14, KJV).[28]

From Mentor Relationship to Traveling Companionship

While my younger self was especially important to me in the years of my transition to older adulthood—during which I perceived him as performing all of the functions of the mentor—my relationship to him has changed in subsequent years. This change has not been accompanied by negative feelings. If anything, my feelings have become even more affectionate. It's simply that I now think of him less as my teacher and more as my faithful companion along life's journey. And here I find our mutual enthusiasm for John Bunyan's *The Pilgrim's Progress* an invaluable

---

26. Ibid., 217.
27. Capps, *The Decades of Life*, 3–41.
28. Erikson, *Identity, Youth and Crisis*, 220.

resource for understanding what we mean to one another.[29] In Bunyan's story, Christian sets forth from his birthplace, the City of Destruction, and eventually arrives at the Celestial City. In the first half of the journey he is accompanied by Faithful, but Faithful is burned at the stake by the city fathers of Vanity Fair because he is having a disruptive effect on its dishonest, greed-driven business practices. Another person, Hopeful, is among the eyewitnesses to the tragic events that occur in Vanity Fair. Inspired by Faithful's witness and also impressed by how Christian "played the man" on this occasion, Hopeful joins Christian on the rest of the journey. He is there to hold Christian's head above water until he feels solid ground underfoot as they cross the River Jordan to the Celestial City.

As my younger self assumed the identity of Christian long before my older self joined the journey, it makes sense to see the two selves as the central character in the story. This, in turn, frees me to think of my younger self as Faithful and my older self as Hopeful, as my older self experiences life much as the young poet who wrote "Winter" does. The fact that older adulthood is often viewed as the winter of life is worth noting in this regard. But more important, I find that in my identity as an older man, I focus more and more on the day at hand and less and less on what lies miles and miles down the road. I also find myself agreeing with the young poet that "this day is the best." This agreement is not based on the fact that I can claim that, after all, I am still here, but on the conviction that the most recent day truly is the best of all. This does not, of course, mean that one should not reminisce about the past out of fear that this will invite invidious comparisons between what was then and what is now. It simply means that intrinsic to hopefulness is the fact that one's basic orientation to life is anticipatory, and central to this anticipatory orientation are the dual affirmations of "This day is best" and "I wish tomorrow would begin."

In the revised version of *The Pilgrim's Progress* that I experience today, Faithful and Hopeful are not identified with successive stages of the journey of life but are traveling together. And this is one of the ways I have experienced growth and development in my older adult years, as I feel the vitality that derives from the feeling that my younger self is with me and that we are like the two travelers on the road to Emmaus. As we

29. Bunyan, *The Pilgrim's Progress*.

walk together, we find ourselves "talking with each other about all these things that had happened" (Luke 24:14).[30]

30. Among my high school writings that came my way following my father's death there was a poem titled "Roads to Emmaus." I discussed this poem briefly in my chapter titled "Close Friendships," in Dykstra et al., *The Faith and Friendships of Teenage Boys*, 100–102.

PART 2

Growth and Development in Older Adulthood

3

The Three Stages of Older Adulthood

. . . . .

*Stage: a period, level, or degree in a process of development,
growth, or change*

. . . . .

As I INDICATED IN the introduction, I will be making the point in this chapter and in chapters 4–5 that older adulthood is a period of growth and development. Since older adulthood is no less a part of the human life cycle than the other parts, the claim that it too is a period of growth and development may seem obvious. This point, however, is rarely mentioned in the literature on older adulthood, and even when it is, it tends to get lost in the larger discussion of the many forces and factors that are arrayed against growth and development. My intention here is not to minimize these forces and factors but rather to recognize that they often contribute to the older adult's growth and development by evoking inner resources—or hidden energies—that one possesses but has not previously had occasion to draw upon.

These chapters will present three different but compatible ways of understanding this growth and development. In this chapter I make the case that older adulthood consists of at least three stages of development, and that these stages, together with the preceding stages, constitute a growth process. In chapter 4 I present the view that the aging process is an ongoing forward movement, and that even the detours or backward steps that occur contribute to growth and life enhancement. In chapter 5 I focus on the topic of creativity among older adults, a topic that enables us to see that older adults experience growth through thinking in constructive ways, in their ways of relating to others, and in their use of gifts, such as a sense of humor, that are not unique to older adults, but that older adults employ in new and creative ways. There are other ways to demonstrate that older adulthood is a period of growth and development, but by focusing on these three ways we will see that growth and development are fundamental to older adulthood and are not limited to a few extraordinary or atypical older adults.

Erik H. Erikson's Life-Cycle Model

In this chapter I will be suggesting that older adulthood consists of at least three developmental stages, and because it does, growth is an integral part of older adulthood. In my discussion of this proposal I will be focusing on Erik H. Erikson's life-cycle model. His is one of the very few such models that are inclusive of the whole developmental process from birth to death. However, in his model, older adulthood is represented as a single stage. This very representation can give the impression that no significant growth occurs in the course of older adulthood. To address this problem, I suggest that there are three developmental stages in older adulthood: the one that he presents in his model and two additional ones. To set the context for this suggestion, we need to take a brief look at his life-cycle model.

Erikson's first presentation of his model was in the chapter titled "The Eight Stages of Man," in *Childhood and Society,* published in 1950.[1] The chapter title was changed to "The Eight Ages of Man" in the revised edition of *Childhood and Society* published in 1963.[2] The model itself has come to be known as a conception of the human "life cycle," a term that suggests that the course of development circles back around to its

1. Erikson, *Childhood and Society* (1st ed.), 219–34.

2. Erikson, *Childhood and Society* (rev. ed.), 247–74. All subsequent quotations in this chapter from *Childhood and Society* are from the revised edition. Erikson changed the title to reflect the speech of Jacques, one of the attending lords of the banished Duke Senior in William Shakespeare's *As You Like It*. It begins: "All the world's a stage, / And all the men and women merely players; / They have their exits and their entrances, / And one man in his time plays many parts, / His acts being seven ages"(44).

beginnings. Because the model has been represented in charts that portray the stages in stairstep fashion, with the stage of infancy at the bottom left and the stage of old age at the top right, the idea of the course of development being cyclical has not received a great deal of attention in discussions of Erikson's model, but in chapter 5 I will propose that the capacities formed in early childhood play a very significant role in the creativity of older adults. This is simply one illustration of the many ways in which we do, in fact, circle back around to life's beginnings, and do so at various stages of life.

Erikson's final presentation of his conception of the life process occurs in his chapter of *The Life Cycle Completed,* published when he was eighty years old, titled "Major Stages in Psychosocial Development."[3] His writings reflect changes in some of their wording over the years, but we may assume that the names of the stages presented in a chart in *The Life Cycle Completed* reflect his final views on the subject.[4] This chart also includes the virtues or human strengths he assigned to the stages.[5] The chart is presented on the following page in table form with an added title and captions.

Since this is a book on older adulthood, I will not discuss the model in detail here. I would simply note that Erikson emphasized the importance of the "ratio" between the positive and the negative psychosocial tendencies central to each stage and the fact that there is a dynamic interplay between these tendencies. In a footnote in the revised edition of *Childhood and Society* Erikson alludes to "certain misuses" of his whole conception of the life cycle. For example, "some writers are so intent on making an *achievement scale* out of these stages that they blithely omit all the 'negative' senses (basic mistrust, etc.) which are and remain the dynamic counterpart of the 'positive' ones throughout life."[6] This discounting of the negative senses falsifies the actual state of affairs, for "the personality is engaged with the hazards of

3. Erikson, *The Life Cycle Completed,* 55–82. This book was originally published in 1982. An extended version of the book was published in 1997, five years after Erikson's death. It contains a new preface and three new chapters written by his wife, Joan M. Erikson. (The original single authorship is retained.) A distinctive feature of *The Life Cycle Completed* is that the chapter on the major stages of psychosocial development presents the stages in reverse order from the eighth to the first stage. All quotations in this chapter are from the extended version.

4. Ibid., 56–57.

5. This "schedule of virtues," as he called it, was originally presented in an essay titled "Human Strength and the Cycle of Generations," published in 1964.

6. Erikson, *Childhood and Society,* 273–74.

Table 3.1: Major Stages in Psychological Development

Stage	Psychosocial Crisis	Virtues
Infancy	Basic Trust vs. Mistrust	Hope
Early Childhood	Autonomy vs. Shame and Doubt	Will
Play Age	Initiative vs. Guilt	Purpose
School Age	Industry vs. Inferiority	Competence
Adolescence	Identity vs. Identity Confusion	Fidelity
Young Adulthood	Intimacy vs. Isolation	Love
Adulthood	Generativity vs. Stagnation	Care
Old Age	Integrity vs. Despair and Disgust	Wisdom

existence continuously, even as the body's metabolism copes with decay," and "as we come to diagnose a state of relative strength and the symptoms of an impaired one, we face only more clearly the paradoxes and tragic potentials of human life."[7]

Furthermore, the "negative" tendency of a given stage can play an important adaptive function, as when a child in the play age (stage 3) feels guilty for hitting or kicking another child. Initiative is a positive thing, but it can also be misused. It should also be noted that in using the word *crisis* to describe the dynamic interplay that occurs between the positive and negative tendencies of a given stage, Erikson does not mean to suggest that this is an inherently negative experience or process. Rather, *crisis* suggests that one has entered a new stage in life that presents not only new challenges but also new opportunities for the development of new or enhanced personal strengths and abilities. Thus, as one enters a new stage the challenge is to develop a ratio between the positive and negative poles that clearly favors the positive.

A Ninth Stage?

In this chapter I will be proposing that we add two additional stages to Erikson's model, making ten in all, and that the additional stages involve an expansion of the model to include not one but three stages in older adulthood.

7. Ibid., 274.

In a conversation with Erikson in 1981 at his home in Tiburon, California, I asked him whether, in the light of increasing longevity, he had considered adding a ninth stage to his eight-stage life-cycle theory. Just then, Joan, his wife, returned home with several bags of groceries. As she put the groceries away, he informed her of some of the things he and I had been discussing in her absence and specifically mentioned my question about a ninth stage. She laughed and immediately went over to a weaving that was hanging in their entryway. It was a weaving of the life-cycle model. She introduces this weaving in the chapter titled "The Woven Life Cycle" in her book *Wisdom and the Senses,* published in 1988. The warp represents the positive or *syntonic* tendencies (trust, autonomy, initiative, and so forth) in various colors, and the woof represents the negative or *dystonic* tendencies in grey.[8] There is an overlapping fringe at the top of the weaving. She pointed to this fringe and said, "These are the fringe benefits!" I believe that she took my question of a possible ninth stage as a reference to the afterlife and, of course, this would be perfectly understandable because she was aware that I was a scholar in religion. But with this bit of humor the issue of another stage was closed.

However, the extended version of Erikson's *The Life Cycle Completed,* published in 1997 (three years after his death) contains a chapter by Joan Erikson titled "The Ninth Stage."[9] In this chapter she notes that when the life-cycle model was originally developed, "it seemed obvious that apart from the infant's arrival date such variety exists in the timing of human development that no age specifications could be validated for each stage independent of social criteria and pressures."[10] However, "while this is also true of old age, it is useful to delineate a specific time frame in order to focus on the life experiences and crises of the period," for "old age in one's eighties and nineties brings with it new demands, reevaluations, and daily difficulties," and "these concerns can only be adequately discussed, and confronted, by designating a new ninth stage to clarify the challenges. We must now see and understand the final life cycle stages through late-eighty and ninety-year-old eyes."[11] Born in

8. Erikson, *Wisdom and the Senses,* 74–112. This chapter places particular emphasis on the virtues assigned to the eight stages and their related colors: *hope* (dark blue), *will* (orange), *purpose* (dark green), *competence* (yellow), *fidelity* (light blue), *love* (rosy red), *care* (light green), and *wisdom* (purple).

9. Erikson, *The Life Cycle Completed,* 105–14.

10. Ibid., 105.

11. Ibid.

1903, she herself was in her nineties when the expanded version of the book was published.

Joan Erikson's ninth stage involves a brief presentation of each of the eight stages but with the positive and negative tendencies reversed. She notes that the positive or systonic tendency "supports growth and expansion, offers goals, celebrates self-respect and commitment of the very finest," and sustains us "as we are challenged by the more dystonic elements with which life confronts us all." In old age, however, we need to recognize "the fact that circumstances may place the dystonic in a more dominant position." Thus, she has placed the negative or dystonic element first "in order to underscore its prominence and potency," but also notes that we need to remember "that conflict and tension are sources of growth, strength, and commitment."[12]

The ensuing pages of "The Ninth Stage" focus on each of the eight psychosocial themes and explore ways in which older adults are confronted with circumstances—physical and social—that cause them to be especially vulnerable to mistrust, shame and doubt, guilt, inferiority, identity confusion, isolation, stagnation, and despair and disgust. She also discusses ways in which older adults continue to draw on the positive tendencies of trust, autonomy, initiative, industry, identity, intimacy, generativity, and integrity but in new and different ways. She concludes her reflections on the eighth stage of the life cycle by noting that the very experience of despair is different in the ninth stage from what it was in the eighth stage. For in the eighth stage—what we may call *early* older adulthood—despair has much to do with an assessment of one's earlier life and the knowledge that it is too late to do anything about it. However, in the ninth stage—of *late* older adulthood—despair is more related to the current struggles of everyday life due to the loss of capacities that one previously possessed.[13]

Here, Joan Erikson presents a viable way of adding a ninth stage to the original life-cycle model without adding an entirely new stage. However, the assumption behind the question I posed to Erik Erikson about the possible need for a ninth stage was that there would be an entirely new stage with a new psychosocial theme. The fact that Joan Erikson does not take this approach is undoubtedly due to various considerations, but foremost among these would be the fact that the *integrity vs. despair and disgust* theme is fundamentally concerned with the *wholeness* of life

12. Ibid., 106.
13. Ibid., 112–14.

itself. This is the stage in which one's life is integrated into a meaningful whole. Such integration may not be entirely successful; for, after all, one also experiences despair and disgust, and these experiences may undermine this very integration. But the fact that integration is the focus of the eighth stage would tend to render an additional stage with its own psychosocial conflict superfluous at best and dysfunctional at worst, as its very existence would seem to threaten the integrity realized in the preceding stage.

The Case for Two Additional Stages

On the other hand, I believe that it makes practical sense to add not just one but two older-adulthood stages to the existing one, making three such stages in all. This belief arose out of an idea that engaged my interest when I was in my sixties, namely, that the eight psychosocial crises in Erikson's life-cycle model might be relocated according to the decades of life. I felt that we might gain new insights into the life process if the stages were distributed differently across the life span but without altering their chronological order. Thus, *Basic Trust vs. Basic Mistrust* would be predominant from birth through nine years of age and *Autonomy vs. Shame and Doubt* would be predominant from age ten through age nineteen, and so forth. I have presented this model in my book *The Decades of Life*.[14] This relocating of the stages according to decades is not intended as a critique of the original locations of the eight stages and the chronological years generally ascribed to each of them. Instead, I think of it as a playful variation on the original model and thus an illustration of how an adult might continue to make use of proclivities developed in the "play age" (stage 3 of Erikson's life-cycle model). This does not, of course, mean that the proposal is not to be taken seriously, for, as Erikson himself frequently pointed out, children take their play constructions with utmost seriousness.[15]

Furthermore, there is a biblical precedent for thinking of our lives in terms of decades. The Bible uses decades to talk about our expected longevity. Gen 6:3 reports: "Then the LORD said, 'My spirit shall not abide in

14. Capps, *The Decades of Life*.

15. As a psychoanalyst of children, Erikson devoted the same careful attention to children's play as his colleagues devoted to adults' dreams. See, for example, Erikson, "Studies in the Interpretation of Play," and Erikson, *Childhood and Society*, chapter 6.

mortals forever, for they are flesh; their days shall be one hundred twenty years'" (NRSV). That's twelve decades. Although Ps 90:10 is not nearly as generous, it too speaks of our expected longevity in terms of decades: "The years of our life are threescore and ten, or even by reason of strength fourscore" (RSV). That's seven or possibly eight decades. The Psalm adds, "Their span is but toil and trouble; they are soon gone, and we fly away," but, for the moment at least, this is beside the point.

If Ps 90:10 says that we can expect to live seven or even eight decades, the relocation of Erikson's eight stages according to decades would conform to the life span that it envisions. But because some persons have even more strength than the psalm considers possible, and live as much as five score years, and sometimes even longer, this means that Erikson's eight-stage model needs to be expanded to include at least two additional stages. The following chart lists Erikson's eight stages with their psychosocial themes and their corresponding virtues plus two additional stages that I propose with their psychosocial crises and virtues.

Table 3.2: The Decades of Life

Chronological Period	Psychological Crisis	Virtue
1–9	Basic Trust vs. Basic Mistrust	Hope
10–19	Autonomy vs. Shame and Doubt	Will
20–29	Initiative vs. Guilt	Purpose
30–39	Industry vs. Inferiority	Competence
40–49	Identity vs. Identity Confusion	Fidelity
50–59	Intimacy vs. Isolation	Love
60–69	Generativity vs. Stagnation	Care
70–79	Integrity vs. Despair and Disgust	Wisdom
80–89	Release vs. Control	Gracefulness
90–99	Desire vs. Struggle	Endurance

Because the two additional stages are my own creation, I realize that they do not have the same authority of Erikson's eight stages. But perhaps, all in all, this is a good thing because their very lack of authority gives these stages a certain amount of flexibility that older adults themselves may appreciate and welcome. An older adult can view these stages—and the decades that they represent—as invitations to improvisation.

In the following discussion of Erikson's stage of *Integrity vs. Despair and Disgust* and the two added stages of *Release vs. Control* and *Desire vs. Struggle*, I will assume, as I indicated earlier, that older adulthood begins at age seventy. I will also be suggesting that the issue of *integrity vs. despair and disgust* is predominantly an eighth-decade issue, although, of course, it may continue to play a role in the two subsequent decades. Joan Erikson's suggestion that in one's eighties and nineties there is a shift from a more retrospective understanding of *integrity vs. despair and disgust* to a more contemporary understanding implicitly supports this suggestion.

The Eighth Decade: Integrity vs. Despair and Disgust

As indicated in the above chart, Erikson suggests that the eighth stage of life is one in which we experience the conflict between integrity on the one hand and despair and disgust on the other. Dictionary definitions of *integrity* use words like *complete, unimpaired, wholeness,* and *soundness* to convey its meaning.[16] Erikson's use of the word *integrity* reflects these understandings. In his opening paragraph on the *integrity vs. despair and disgust* stage in *Identity and the Life Cycle,* he emphasizes that integrity represents the culmination of all the preceding stages.[17] Thus, it represents the very *wholeness* of life.

Erikson also identifies some of its attributes. First, it "is the acceptance of one's own and only life cycle and of the people who have become significant to it as something that had to be and that, by necessity, permitted of no substitutions." Thus, it means "a new and different love of one's parents," one that is "free of the wish that they should have been different and an acceptance of the fact that one's life is one's own responsibility."[18] The key word here is *acceptance. Acceptance* may suggest a sense of resignation (as when one *accepts* defeat), but it may also mean approval or a favorable reception (as when a student *accepts* a grade that was higher than expected).[19] Thus, *acceptance* of "one's own and only life cycle" could

---

16. Agnes et al., eds., *Webster's New World College Dictionary,* 742.

17. Erikson, *Identity and the Life Cycle,* 98.

18. Ibid.

19. Agnes et al., eds., *Webster's New World College Dictionary,* 8.

range from feeling that although one was dealt a bad hand it could have been much worse to believing that one has truly been blessed.

Second, integrity "is a sense of comradeship with men and women of distant times and of different pursuits, who have created orders and objects and sayings conveying human dignity and love."[20] A *comrade* is a friend or close companion, or a person who shares interests and activities in common with others.[21] Thus, Erikson is suggesting that integrity involves friendship or companionship with persons who lived many years—even centuries—ago, but whose lives reflect the values that one holds dear.

Third, although one is aware of the relativity of all the various lifestyles that have given meaning to human striving, one is ready to defend one's own lifestyle as legitimate and meaningful.[22] Thus, if the second attribute of this state of mind emphasizes the connection between one's own life and those of men and women of long ago, the third attribute affirms the essential validity of one's own lifestyle, and does not treat some historical form or expression of integrity as the norm against which it is to be evaluated and judged. A life of integrity is possible in every generation, and by claiming the integrity of the style of life that one has lived, one implicitly affirms the integrity of the lives of our ancestors, however different they were from ours.

But integrity does not exist in an ivory tower. It has to contend with *despair* and *disgust*. Drawing on his understanding of *integrity* as "the acceptance of one's own and only life cycle," Erikson suggests that when *despair* prevails, such acceptance is not forthcoming, for it "expresses the feeling that time is short, too short for the attempt to start another life and to try out alternate roads to integrity." Also, despair "is often hidden behind a show of disgust" or "a chronic contemptuous displeasure with particular institutions and particular people," and such outward expressions of disgust and displeasure may disguise feelings of self-contempt.[23]

---

20. Erikson, *Identity and the Life Cycle*, 98.

21. Agnes et al., eds., *Webster's New World College Dictionary*, 300.

22. Erikson, *Identity and the Life Cycle*, 98.

23. Ibid.

The Virtue of Wisdom

Erikson identifies wisdom as the virtue or human strength of the *integrity vs. despair and disgust* stage of the life cycle. Dictionary definitions of *wisdom* emphasize "judgment," especially good judgment in deciding upon a course of action that is fundamentally sound because it reflects understanding of the situation based on experience and knowledge.[24] Wisdom is therefore not equated with esoteric knowledge or abstract theorizing. Rather, it is practical, sensible, and capable of explaining why it recommends one course of action over others. Erikson suggests that we find in older persons forms and expressions of wisdom that reflect "all of its connotations from ripened 'wits' to accumulated knowledge and matured judgment. It is the essence of knowledge freed from temporal relativity." He adds that such wisdom "maintains and conveys the integrity of experience, in spite of the decline of bodily and mental functions."[25] To be sure,

> potency, performance, and adaptability decline; but if vigor of mind combines with the gift of responsible renunciation, some old people can envisage human problems in their entirety (which is what "integrity" means) and can represent to the coming generation a living example of the "closure" of a style of life. Only such integrity can balance the despair of the knowledge that a limited life is coming to a conscious conclusion [and] only such wholeness can transcend the petty disgust of feeling finished and passed by, and the despair of facing the period of relative helplessness which marks the end as it marked the beginning.[26]

Erikson concludes his reflections on wisdom with the observation that some persons seem to be especially gifted as representatives of wisdom. There are the leaders and thinkers "who round out long productive lives in positions in which wisdom is of the essence and is of service," and there are those "who feel verified in numerous and vigorous progeny." But, eventually, they, too, will join the very old, "who are reduced to a narrow space-time, in which only a few things, in their self-contained form, offer a last but firm whisper of confirmation."[27]

24. Agnes et al., eds., *Webster's New World College Dictionary,* 1643.

25. Erikson, "Human Strength and the Cycle of Generations," 133.

26. Ibid., 134.

27. Ibid.

Studies of Older Adults

Erikson wrote an article on *Wild Strawberries* by the Swedish filmmaker Ingmar Bergman for a book he was editing on the subject of adulthood.[28] This film focuses on an old Swedish doctor's trip from his home in northern Sweden to the southern city of Lund in order to receive an honorary doctorate at the University of Lund. I will not discuss Erikson's article here but simply note that Dr. Borg was seventy-six years old. Since Erikson was born in 1902 and the article was published in 1978, we may assume that Erikson was about the same age as the film's main character when he was writing the article. In fact, he notes in the article that in light of his annual use of the film in his undergraduate course at Harvard on the human life cycle, students have expressed the "friendly suspicion" that he personally identified with the central character in the film. Erikson dismisses what he considers the more superficial associations that students had made between himself and Dr. Borg, but he acknowledges that there is a sense in which one's "conception of the whole of life" cannot "transcend the observations and values that are part of our own limited existence."[29] He does not say whether he believes this is a good thing or a bad thing, but he makes an important point here, namely, that he does not view his life-cycle model as a purely scientific construct but rather a way of seeing the human life span: it represents a view that, from his own personal perspective, has its own integrity. When Erikson was in his early twenties, he aspired to be an artist. I believe that his life-cycle model is a work of art and that this how he viewed it himself.

On the other hand, Erikson was a practicing clinician, and it was important to him that his life-cycle model reflect the experience of real, living persons. In this regard, it is noteworthy that he participated in an empirically oriented study of older adults when he himself was in his early eighties. The results of this study are presented in *Vital Involvement in Old Age,* by Erik and Joan Erikson and Helen Kivnick.[30] Helen Kivnick was an associate professor at the California School of Professional Psychology in Berkeley and a practicing clinical psychologist at the time, and Erik and Joan Erikson were living in Tiburon, California, which is in the San Francisco Bay Area. Erik Erikson was eighty-four years old, and Joan Erikson was eighty-five years old when the book was published. The

28. Erikson, "Reflections on Dr. Borg's Life Cycle."
29. Ibid. 4.
30. Erikson et al., *Vital Involvement in Old Age.*

older adults who were the subjects of the study were the parents of the children in their early teens who had been studied several decades earlier by the Guidance Study Project of the Institute of Human Development of the University of California at Berkeley. As a member of the research team in the 1940s, Erikson had summarized fifty of the 248 teenagers' life histories. This was also the decade when he formulated his life-cycle model. In 1981 funding from the National Institute of Mental Health, under the auspices of the Rehabilitation Research and Training Center on Aging at the University of Pennsylvania, made it possible to study the parents of the Guidance Study children, all of whom were now over fifty years old. The twenty-nine parents now ranged from seventy-five to ninety-five years of age. Erik and Joan Erikson and Helen Kivnick visited their homes.[31]

I will simply present here what the authors identified as aspects or features of *integrity* and *despair* in their conversations with the subjects of their study. Six ways of realizing or maintaining integrity were mentioned by one or more persons:

1. Looking for guidance from the elders one has held in highest esteem from one's early years (for example, a parent or grandparent), or from another person whom one admires (for example, a celebrity, a neighbor, or a Good Samaritan at a senior center).

2. Increasing concern for and tolerance of the world and its multifarious inhabitants as reflected in greater patience, open-mindedness, understanding, and compassion, and in the ability to see both sides of an issue. Interestingly enough, some indicated that being "more set in one's ways" need not be inconsistent with greater tolerance toward others because they recognized that their own insistence on their preferred ways of doing things made them more tolerant of other people when they insisted on doing things *their* way.

3. Developing a philosophy of aging (which included continuing to grow and not allowing oneself to stagnate), committing energetically to a daily routine, remaining actively involved with other people,

31. Fourteen of the twenty-nine participants in the study lived in their own homes (the homes where they lived when their children were growing up), six lived in retirement communities, five lived in small private apartments, one woman lived in her daughter's home, one man lived alone in a small cabin, and one couple lived in a government-subsidized partial-care facility.

acting on one's need to be needed, and maintaining a sense of humor, especially about oneself.

4. Turning to religion, which included church and synagogue participation, the recollection of engagement in religious observances as a child, and affirming the importance of the ritualized community that churches and synagogues represent.

5. Acknowledging and accepting one's past choices. This included ascribing new meaning to earlier experiences that were painful, and accepting the fact that earlier decisions cannot be altered now.

6. Integrating legitimate feelings of cynicism and hopelessness into a larger perspective that is more accepting and hopeful.

The following grounds for despair were also mentioned:

1. The fact that others their age were leaving the community where they had spent much of their lives together.

2. Largely involuntary thoughts about dying, not feeling well, getting depressed and feeling "somehow let down."

3. Necessary thinking about the future occurring in the context of the realization that death may not be very far off.

4. The sense that the future of the world is not as good as its past, together with the realization that one cannot do much if anything about it.

5. Ruminating over one's earlier powerlessness to save a loved one from dying, and thinking of what one might have done differently.

6. Being obligated to provide material assistance to family members when they should be capable of taking care of their own affairs.

Finally, strategies for maintaining integrity over despair were identified:

1. Taking a viable personal future for granted by involving oneself in activities that assume one has several or even many productive years ahead.

2. Taking interest in one's grandchildren as representatives of a future that not only extends beyond one's own future but also that of one's own children.

3. Emulating an older person, especially a family member, who exemplified mental vigor and emotional strength when he or she was
   one's current age.

4. Minimizing or even ignoring the painful experiences or questionable decisions in earlier stages of life. The three authors were aware
   that this was being done because there were extensive files on the
   children of these parents.

We might view this fourth strategy as a form of denial or even dis-
honesty, but it is worth recalling here the fact that Joseph reframed the
experience of being sold into slavery by telling his remorseful brothers
that God meant it for good, so that the lives of many people would be
saved (Gen 45:1–8). Of course, we would view their reunion very differently if the brothers themselves had made this point to Joseph in order to
rationalize and justify their earlier mistreatment of him.[32]

This brief summary of the results of the study indicate that older
adults *do* in fact struggle with the issue of *integrity vs. despair* and seek
ways to maintain a positive ratio between the two components of this
psychosocial crisis. Also, the fact that the subjects of the study ranged
from seventy-five to ninety-five indicates that maintaining a positive ratio of *integrity* over *despair* remains an important concern throughout
one's older adulthood. However, I believe that the *integrity vs. despair* crisis is especially prominent in an older person's seventies, and that other
psychosocial crises come more to the fore in their eighties and nineties.
Thus, we turn now to the ninth and tenth decades and the psychosocial
crises that I have assigned to them.

The Ninth Decade: Release vs. Control

I suggest that persons in their eighties experience the conflict of *release
vs. control*. According to the dictionary, *release* has many meanings, including (1) "to set free, as from confinement, duty or work"; (2) "to let
go or let loose, as to *release* an arrow"; (3) "to grant freedom from a tax,
penalty or obligation"; (4) "to give up or surrender a claim"; (5) "relief
from pain or cares"; (6) "relief from emotional tension through a spontaneous, uninhibited expression of an emotion"; and (7) "the act of letting

32. See Rotenberg, "The 'Midrash' and Biographic Rehabilitation." See also Furman and Ahola's discussion of the past as a resource in *Solution Talk,* 18–37.

loose something caught or held in position."[33] There is also the idea of *released time,* which means being freed from one's regular duties in order to pursue other tasks or activities. *Release* may also refer to a capsule whose medicinal effect is sustained over a relatively long time period.

There is an interesting dynamic in the meanings that concern granting freedom from a tax, penalty, or obligation; and giving up or surrendering a claim. If these happen to concern two individuals, the act of the first person *releases* the second person from having to make good on an obligation, but it also *releases* the first person from having to persuade or coerce the other to do so. I think that Jesus has something like this second form of *release* in mind when he advises his listeners: if someone takes away your goods, do not ask for them again (Luke 6:30b [cf. NRSV]).

Clearly, *release* is a word with many nuances, but they all suggest, in one way or another, that *release* stands in opposition to *control.* According to the dictionary, *control* means "to exercise authority over another," "to regulate," and "to hold back, curb or restrain." These various meanings suggest that *control* can be imposed by others, but that it can also be self-imposed, as when we make an effort to restrain our emotions. The same is true of *release.* Others may decide not to impose taxes, penalties, or obligations that they have a right to impose, but we can also *release* ourselves from a self-imposed restriction, as when we express an emotion in a spontaneous, uninhibited manner. Thus, *release* and *control* may apply to our relations with others, but they may also apply to what occurs within us.

A meaning of *release* that can have particular relevance for persons in their eighties is relief from pain and cares, and this meaning may have a direct corollary in the definition of *control* as regulative, especially in the sense of medicinal substances and medical treatments that regulate physical pain. These particular meanings of *release* and *control* suggest that one needs a ratio of *release* and *control* that favors *release* but this does not mean that all *control* is to be avoided, challenged, or condemned.

The Virtue of Gracefulness

I suggest that *gracefulness* is the virtue or human strength that assumes an important role in the ninth decade of life. The dictionary defines *graceful* as "having grace or beauty of form, composition, movement,

---

33. Agnes et al., eds., *Webster's New World College Dictionary,* 1210.

or expression; elegant."[34] The word *graceful* makes us think of ballet dancers or gazelles. But there is also the fact that the word *gracefulness* contains the word *grace*. This word is such a familiar one that it may seem unnecessary to cite its dictionary definitions, but these definitions remind us of its multiplicity of meanings. They include "beauty or charm of form, composition, movement or expression," "a sense of what is right and proper," "thoughtfulness toward others," "goodwill" or favor," "mercy or clemency," "a period of time granted beyond the date set for the performance of an act or payment of an obligation," "a short prayer in which thanks are given for a meal," and several theological meanings, including "the unmerited love and favor of God toward mankind," "divine influence acting in a person to make the person pure or morally strong," "the condition of a person brought to God's favor through this influence," and "a special virtue, gift or help given to a person by God."[35]

These definitions of the word *grace* include the idea of beauty of form, composition, movement, or expression, but several others relate to interactions between persons, ranging from having a sense of what is right and proper to allowing another person more time to fulfill a commitment. In the academic world, we call these extensions. Thus, even before God comes into the picture, there are several ways in which *grace* manifests itself in the manner in which we relate to one another. When we get to the theological definitions, we come upon the idea that this is how God relates to us.

For our purposes here, I would like to retain the aesthetic meaning of *gracefulness* because it has metaphorical importance even for those of us who could hardly claim to be physically graceful, and it suggests that there can be a certain beauty in the way we relate to one another with simple, everyday thoughtfulness. But how does the virtue or human strength of gracefulness relate to the *release vs. control* conflict? The most obvious connection is the definition of *release* as the granting of freedom from a tax, penalty, or obligation, and the definition of *grace* as a period of time granted beyond the date or time set for the performance of an act or payment of an obligation. Granting a grace period for meeting an obligation does not go as far as releasing a person from the obligation altogether, but both reflect the desire of the person who grants it to make

34. Ibid., 615.
35. Ibid., 614–15.

a thoughtful gesture likely to produce or create in the other person a deep sense of relief. Neither act has the implication of condescension toward or condemnation of the other; instead, they suggest that the grantors are in a secure enough position themselves that they can afford the luxury, as it were, of not strictly holding the other to a prior agreement.

A deeper if more subtle connection between the virtue of gracefulness and the *release vs. control* conflict is reflected in the metaphorical meaning of *gracefulness*. If we think of the ballet dancer or the gazelle as exhibiting gracefulness, we sense that their beauty of form, composition, movement, and expression involve an ideal relationship *between* release and control. Neither relies exclusively on release, for beauty of form is not merely a matter of "letting loose" with all sorts of physical movements, gyrations, and the like. An indiscriminant flapping of arms and wiggling or shaking of legs will hardly be mistaken for gracefulness. The exercise of control is essential for the physical release, the graceful movement of the gazelle across the fields and hills and valleys.

Something like this physical relationship between release and control may also serve as a spiritual ideal—one that is especially relevant in the ninth decade of life when a person is likely to be experiencing difficulties in maintaining the physical ideal. Many an eighty-year-old has said of a particular physical movement of theirs—"That wasn't very graceful, was it?"—but the very awareness that one may be struggling to maintain a certain physical gracefulness may direct our attention to the possibilities, for oneself and for others, inherent in the capacity for a spiritual gracefulness that reflects an ideal relationship between release and control. In Erikson's own terminology, this implies a certain "ratio" between them that favors release but also recognizes the value of the moderating effects of control.

Relinquishing Control

As I have suggested, release and control are not necessarily adversaries. In fact, release often has meaning and significance only when it occurs in relationship with control, as when one is granted freedom from a tax, penalty, or obligation, or when something that has been caught or held in position is let loose. Without control, it wouldn't make much sense to talk about release. If a prison has no locks, and inmates are free to come and go as they please, to speak of being released from prison would be rather meaningless.

But the fact that release gets its meaning from its relationship to control does not mean that control is necessarily or invariably a good thing in itself. In fact, we often insist on the necessity of control when there is no need for it, or we emphasize the need for control in our lives because the human or social environment in which we live seems utterly chaotic. It is also true that older adults can sometimes be overly controlling toward others, perhaps as a reaction to experiences in which they had to relinquish their own autonomy over one or another aspect of their lives. A common pair of themes in the lives of persons in their eighties (and often earlier) concerns the control that family members exercise over them and, conversely, the control they exercise over family members. A son, daughter, or other family member may insist that they leave their homes and enter a care facility when they would much prefer to stay put. On the other hand, they may exercise control over family members through decisions about how their money and possessions will be distributed after their death. These decisions are typically revealed in advance to their various beneficiaries, often with the intention of exercising control over their behavior. Of course, determining how to distribute one's money and possessions in a way that is equitable, fair, and loving is often a difficult task, one somewhat akin to walking through a minefield. But to the extent possible, one would hope that this might be an occasion in which the ratio of release to control is overwhelmingly on the side of the release, and where the virtue of gracefulness is such a commanding presence that the vices of greed, jealousy, and anger go scurrying for cover.

The Tenth Decade: Desire vs. Struggle

I suggest that persons in their nineties experience the conflict of desire vs. struggle. The dictionary defines *desire* as "wishing or longing for," but also as "craving and coveting."[36] It compares the word *desire* with the words *wish*, *want*, and *crave*, noting that *desire* is generally interchangeable with these other words in the sense that all of them involve "a longing for." But *desire* conveys an intensity or ardor not expressed as strongly in the word *wish*, which has the connotation of an unrealizable longing—such

36. Ibid., 391.

as the wish that summer were already here; while the word *want* conveys the sense of a longing for something that one lacks; and the word *crave* suggests an urgent longing.[37]

Thus, the idea behind the word *desire* is that we believe the object of our desire is realizable and is no fleeting or inconsequential matter. When I was a college student, I was greatly impressed by the title of Bach's "Jesu, Joy of Man's Desiring": so much so that when my wife and I were planning our wedding, I suggested that we ask the soloist to sing it. He agreed, but only if we let him sing it in German, a surprising request to which we readily agreed. What especially impressed me was the fact that the title contained the word *desiring*, which conveyed an *enduring* sentiment, and not a mere wish or want or craving.

The *desire* that exists inside the hearts, minds, and spirits of persons in their nineties is very similar to the desire expressed in the title of Bach's hymn arrangement: such desire is more enduring than a wish, less urgent than a craving, and less a response to something one lacks than to something one has and does not want to lose. This is the *desire* for life itself. Although individual ninety-year-olds may have very different views and understandings of what is life for them, their *desire* is for life. This does not mean that one no longer has wishes, wants, and cravings, but life itself is what desire is fundamentally about.

This *desire*, however, comes up against the inevitable *struggle* often experienced long before one reaches ninety, but that becomes unavoidable in one's nineties. The dictionary defines *struggle* as "contending or fighting against an opponent," "making great efforts or attempts," and "making one's way with difficulty, as through a thicket."[38] The third definition seems tailor-made for persons in their nineties, for many ninety-year-olds make their way with difficulty and may even find the illustration of struggling through a thicket an appropriate metaphor. This "thicket" may take the form of a congeries of doctor's offices and hospitals, the routines of the social environment of an assisted-living facility, and even, perhaps, the gathering thicket that one may feel inside one's head.

The second definition of *struggle* is also relevant. Persons in their nineties find it necessary to make great efforts or attempts especially in learning how to do the hard way what they previously did with relative ease. For example, there are the six standard activities of daily living that

37. Ibid., 391.
38. Ibid., 1421.

are used as a basis for determining whether a person qualifies for long-term health care benefits: bathing, dressing, eating, continence, transferring, and toileting. There are also the host of changes in one's physical condition that may not fall under any one of these criteria, that yet make one's daily life a challenge: ringing in one's ears, changes in visual acuity that make it difficult to read or drive a car, or inability to climb a flight of stairs because one's back or knees or hips, or heart will not cooperate. Social interaction may also require "great efforts or attempts." One may find it a struggle to react quickly to sudden changes in one's social environment when, for example, one's children and grandchildren come to visit, or when one is moved from one nursing home to another or from one room to another room with a different configuration and outside view.

As for the first definition of *struggle* ("contending against an opponent"), the fact that desire is the struggle for life itself leads naturally to the conclusion that the opponent is death. This opponent is sometimes the consequence of an external agency (as in the case of a tornado or fire). But it may also be an internal agency (as in the case of heart failure). It is interesting to note in this regard that Sigmund Freud proposed in his small book *Beyond the Pleasure Principle*,[39] originally published in 1920 when he was sixty-four years old, that we have two basic instincts or drives within ourselves. One is the drive to maintain and sustain our life. The other is the drive to end or terminate our life. These two drives contend with each other.

The idea that we have an inherent instinct for keeping ourselves alive seems indisputable. But the idea that we have an instinct for terminating our life was one that even Freud's closest colleagues found difficult to accept. In fact, Freud had questions about the idea himself, so he presented the idea with a great deal of tentativeness, even saying at one point in the book that it would be perfectly all right with him if readers felt he was merely playing devil's advocate.[40] But the idea had come to him when he was thinking about the fact that some of our instincts obey the pressure for novelty and unprecedented experience while others obey the pressure to repeat what we have already experienced time and time again. Some of this repetition may be pleasurable, as when a child begs for the retelling of a story exactly as it was told before; but some of this repetition seems to have a different purpose, as it brings no sense of pleasure. It seems, rather,

39. Freud, *Beyond the Pleasure Principle*.
40. Ibid., 103.

to favor inertia, a tendency to remain in the same fixed condition without change or movement.

Freud reasoned that this second form of repetition is a sort of living death, and that it may be the outward expression of a deeper instinct for not living at all, of falling into a deep sleep from which one does not awaken. Thus, we seem to have a silent death drive that seeks to reduce living matter to an inorganic condition and wants to end the existence of the organism in its own way—not by something done *to* it, such as homicide, a fatal accident, a virus, food poisoning, and so forth, but by some internal process that overcomes the instinct for life and effects a permanent state of inertia or death.

As I have indicated, when Freud wrote *Beyond the Pleasure Principle*, he wasn't entirely convinced that it was a sound idea. But by 1924, four years after the book was published, he employed the two-basic-drives idea in an article, and did so quite casually, as though there wasn't anything controversial about it at all.[41] Freud never wavered from the idea after that.[42] His certainty may have been due to his own physical struggles. He began experiencing a painful swelling on his palate in 1917 due to a long-standing addiction to cigar smoking, and by early 1923 a cancerous growth had developed on his palate and jaw.[43] The book about the two drives was published in 1920, midway between the painful swelling and the cancerous growth six years later. The growth was surgically removed, but it returned at various times in subsequent years, and by 1939, several cancerous lesions in his jaw were causing what he called "paralyzing pain," and his ulcerated cancer wound gave off such a disagreeable smell that his dog would cringe from him and could not be lured into his presence.[44]

Why would Freud's struggle with cancer convince him that the idea we have a silent death drive within ourselves was really true? The answer is relatively simple: A cancer is a group of cells (usually derived from a single cell) that has lost its normal control mechanisms and therefore grows in an unregulated manner. These cells can develop from any tissue in the body and can spread from their initial site throughout the body. Cancerous cells develop from healthy cells in a complex process called transformation, which may occur spontaneously or be brought on by a

41. Freud, "The Economic Problem of Masochism."
42. Gay, *Freud,* 402.
43. Ibid., 420–21.
44. Ibid., 640–49.

cancer-causing agent or carcinogen. Carcinogens include many chemi-
cals, tobacco, viruses, radiation, and sunlight. But not all cells are equally
susceptible to carcinogens. A genetic flaw in a cell may make it more
susceptible.[45]

Thus, the ultimate cause of death in Freud's case was a form of
growth within the body that was no longer *regulated*. We normally think
of growth as conducive to life, but cancer is a type of growth that destroys
life. Thus, we can see how Freud's awareness that he was in danger of
developing a malignant cancer together with his awareness that he was
reluctant to change his lifestyle in the face of this danger would lead him
to propose that we have within ourselves a silent death drive. Our minds
are trying to reconcile two different laws: one devoted to life, and the
other equally devoted to death.

Whether we have a drive toward death or not, the very fact that the
phrase "rest in peace" is inscribed on gravestones, that we sing hymns
at funerals which declare that the struggle is over and the strife is done,
and that we reassure ourselves that our loved one has entered a peaceful
sleep, suggests that we do not view inertia as an unmitigated evil. There
are times and situations where we think it best to allow a loved one to
enter a deep and lasting sleep and not be forced to awaken again. And
even though we tend to think of death as an external force—an enemy we
name Death, who may even have his own residence (we say a person is
"at death's door")—death is actually the conclusion of an internal process
in which one's vital organs cease to function.

If these things are true, then it seems appropriate to view the
struggle that occurs in one's nineties (if not earlier) as one in which the
conflict between desire and struggle is more internal than external. En-
vironmental factors certainly play a role in this struggle, but the nineties
are a decade in which one's struggles have mainly to do with what is going
on *inside* one's body and mind. And this brings us to the virtue or human
strength of endurance.

The Virtue of Endurance

The dictionary defines *endurance* as "the ability to last, continue and
remain; the ability to stand pain, distress and fatigue; and duration." It
defines *to endure* as "to hold up under pain, and fatigue, etc."; and "to

45. Beers, ed., *The Merck Manual of Medical Information,* 1031.

put up with or tolerate." It defines *enduring* as "lasting and remaining," "bearing pain, etc, without flinching," and "holding out."[46]

The very fact that a person has lived into the tenth decade of life suggests that he or she has a proven capacity to continue in existence, the ability to last and remain. Many factors are responsible for why some persons live into their nineties and others do not, and the majority of these factors are outside one's own control or ability to influence. But those who *do* make it to ninety often marvel at the fact that they are still around while so many of their contemporaries are not. For some it's a blessing, for others a curse, and for most it's a *mixed* blessing—good in some ways, not so good in others—or they say that it *would* have been a blessing if only their beloved companion were here to share the nineties with them.

But simple duration is not what makes endurance a virtue. What makes it a virtue is how one expresses or exhibits the *power* of enduring, especially in the ability to stand pain, distress, and fatigue, and the *strength* to put up with or tolerate what is happening and what is being done to oneself. The Apostle Paul has some very positive things to say about endurance in this regard. In his letter to the Christians in Rome he said that "we rejoice in our sufferings, knowing that suffering produces *endurance,* and *endurance* produces character, and character produces hope" (Rom 5:3–4 RSV). In his letter to the Christians in Corinth he noted that "love bears all things, believes all things, hopes all things, *endures* all things" (1 Cor 13:7 RSV).

In both cases, *endurance* has an association with hope, the virtue that Erikson assigns to the first stage of life. In fact, Erikson makes a connection between endurance and hope when he points out that hope is verified by a critical acquisition in infancy, namely, "the secure apperception of an 'object.'"[47] He notes that psychoanalysts think of this as the first "love-object," and note the infant's experience of the care-taking person as a *coherent being,* while genetic psychologists "mean by this the ability to perceive the *enduring quality of the thing world.*"[48] Hope, then, is based on the sense that the external world—or some object within it—possesses the capacity to endure: the ability to hold on, to hold up, and to hold out.

This way of thinking about the connection between the virtues of endurance and hope enables us to see that the ninety-year-old person's endurance is not based on personal fortitude alone, for it also depends

46. Agnes et al., eds., *Webster's New World College Dictionary,* 470.

47. Erikson, "Human Strength and the Cycle of Generations," 116.

48. Ibid., 116–17.

on the reciprocity or mutuality between oneself and an "object" in the external world. And this brings us back to desire, the positive tendency of this decade of life.

Desire differs from mood (like happiness or sadness), attitude (like friendliness or unfriendliness), or temperament (like optimism or pessimism) because a person may express or exhibit a mood, attitude, or temperament without expecting any reciprocal response from anyone or anything in the world. Not so with desire, for desire is inherently relational. The dictionary says that the word *desire* is derived from the Latin word *desiderate,* which means "to await from the stars."[49] *What* is awaited is not specified, but *that* we expect an act or response is an essential feature of *desire*. If there is no response, we have desired in vain.

Desire: The Engine of Life

One of the most well-known sayings in Ecclesiastes (one of the major books of wisdom in the Bible) is the admonition to "Remember your creator in the days of your youth" (12:1a). When I was a teenager, this admonition was often the basis for sermons to us kids at youth camp. The rest of the passage was never cited, probably because it was felt to be irrelevant to teenagers, too despairing, or both. Here it is in full (12:1–7 NRSV), and presented in poetic form:

> Remember your creator in the days of your youth,
> before the days of trouble come, and the years draw near
> when you will say, "I have no pleasure in them";
> before the sun and the light and the moon and the stars
> are darkened and the clouds return with the rain;
>
> in the day when the guards of the house tremble,
> and the strong men are bent, and the women
> who grind cease working because they are few,
> and those who look through the windows see dimly;
>
> when the doors on the street are shut,
> and the sound of the grinding is low,
> and one rises up at the sound of a bird,
> and all the daughters of song are brought low;

49. Agnes et al., eds., *Webster's New World College Dictionary,* 391.

when one is afraid of heights, and terrors are in the road;
the almond tree blossoms, the grasshopper drags itself along,
and desire fails; because all must go to their eternal home,
and the mourners will go about the streets;

before the silver cord is snapped, and the golden bowl is broken,
and the pitcher is broken at the fountain, and the wheel
broken at the cistern, and the dust returns to the earth
as it was, and the breath returns to God who gave it.

In *Words of Delight*, Leland Ryken suggests that this is a highly met-aphorical depiction of old age. The image "the sun and the light and the moon and the stars are darkened" refers to weak eyesight. "Clouds [that] return after the rain" is an allusion to tears from eyestrain. "The keepers of the house that tremble" are shaking hands and arms, "the strong men that are bent" are stooping shoulders, and the loss of teeth is figuratively described as "grinders cease because they are few." Weak eyes are pictured in the figure of windows that are dimmed, weak hearing is evoked by "the doors on the street that are shut," the "almond tree [that] blossoms" relates to white hair, and the allusion to "the grasshopper [that] drags it-self along" refers to the loss of sprightliness in walking.[50] In this account, white hair seems the one positive thing about aging, and Proverbs 20:29 concurs: "The glory of youths is their strength, but the beauty of the aged is their gray hair" (NRSV).

Even if Ryken were mistaken about certain specific images and their metaphorical meanings, the poet is obviously thinking about advanced age. He admonishes readers to "remember your creator in the days of your youth, / before the days of trouble come, and the years draw near / when you will say, 'I have no pleasure in them.'" Moreover, a specific indication of the poem's relevance to the *desire vs. struggle* conflict in the tenth decade of life is its suggestion that in old age "the grasshopper drags itself along and *desire fails*" (12:5). No wonder, then, that the mourners appear on the streets, and that there is evidence—in the snapping of the silver cord, the breaking of the golden bowl, the pitcher, and the wheel at the cistern—that one's world appears to be disintegrating all around oneself. It's as though the mind, which may itself be disintegrating, no longer perceives the object world as having the quality of endurance. This poem, then, emphasizes the preeminence of struggle over desire. In fact,

50. Ryken, *Words of Delight*, 326–28.

it suggests that the time will come when there is no reason to endure and nothing to be desired.

However, a poem by Stanley Kunitz, who was at least ninety years old when he wrote it, challenges the idea that desire itself might fail. Instead, desire is never extinguished for good, for it is always on the alert for the revivifying touch of another.[51] The first line is from his poem "As Flowers Are,"[52] a poem he had written forty years earlier.

Touch Me

Summer is late, my heart.
Words plucked out of the air
some forty years ago
when I was wild with love
and torn almost in two
scatter like leaves this night
of whistling wind and rain.
It is my heart that's late,
it is my song that's flown.
Outdoors all afternoon
under a gunmetal sky
staking my garden down,
I kneeled to the crickets trilling
underfoot as if about
to burst from their crusty shells;
and like a child again
marveled to hear so clear
and brave a music pour
from such a small machine.
What makes the engine go?
Desire, desire, desire.
The longing for the dance
stirs in the buried life.
One season only,
and it's done.
So let the battered old willow

51. Kunitz, *The Collected Poems*, 266.
52. Ibid., 92.

thrash against the windowpanes
and the house timbers creak.
Darling, do you remember
the man you married? Touch me,
remind me who I am.

Roger Housden wrote about this poem in his article "One Life, One Season." Noting that the crickets are trilling their mating song, he observes:

> It is late summer for Kunitz, too, and he is keenly aware that his last days are all too near. But does that mean he has nothing to do? Far from it. The marvelous thing in this poem is that Kunitz realizes his season lasts for the duration of his lifetime. The desire, the engine of his life, will continue until his dying breath. Knowing this, he is not afraid.[53]

Thus, we have in this poem the personal testimony of a man in his nineties that desire does not fail. This does not mean, of course, that the poem in Ecclesiastes is wrong about desire, for surely there are those for whom desire eventually fails. But if the author of Ecclesiastes can invoke the grasshopper that drags itself along in support of its view, Kunitz has just as much right to invoke the cricket in support of his: desire itself endures, and because it does, we can put into perspective the fact that the battered old willow thrashes against the windowpanes and that the house timbers creak. These sounds and rumblings may be true, but if we listen closely, we can hear the trilling of the little engines underfoot. In doing so, we become children again, and this, after all, is one of the blessings of growing old.

Conclusion

I have considered naming the conflict that persons in the eleventh (100–109) and twelfth (110–119) decades of life experience. These names might reflect the fact that the overwhelming majority of persons over one hundred are women.[54] But I have not carried through on this consideration for several reasons. One is that persons who have survived this long have a fundamental right to do their own naming of the conflict that they

53. Housdon, "One Life, One Season," 37.
54. See Capps and Carlin, "Methuselah and Company."

experience in their eleventh or twelve decades of life without interference from those of us who are simply awestruck by the fact that they have lived so long. Another is that the conflict that prevails in one's nineties—of desire vs. struggle—may well retain its prominence in subsequent decades. If this is so, what seems especially true of persons who have lived into the second century of their lives is that they give form and substance to our own affinity with the persons of faith of whom the author of Hebrews writes when he says that they—as strangers and exiles—were seeking a homeland, but not the one that they had left behind. For "if they had been thinking of that land from which they had gone out, they would have had opportunity to return. But as it is, they desire a better country, that is, a heavenly one" (Heb 11:16). For them, desire did not fail. Instead, it envisioned a home, a country, that they had hopes of occupying when their struggles in *this* life were over.

However, the central reason for my not feeling the need to name these decades is that I believe that the addition of two stages to Erikson's stage makes the point that older adulthood is a period of ongoing growth and development. The division of these stages into clearly defined decades is not the important thing. What *is* important is the idea that these additional stages convey that older adulthood is not a period of some thirty years or more in which there is little growth and development. On the contrary, there is as much growth and development in these decades of life as there was in earlier decades of life. Moreover, as Erikson has pointed out, the psychosocial crises at each stage of the life cycle reflect the changing circumstances to which an individual is subject in the course of life. As we will see in chapter 4, these changing circumstances invite, or even require, a creative response, and there is ample evidence that older adults possess the internal resources, some of which were developed in early childhood, that enable them to respond effectively to the challenge.

4

The Aging Process as Forward Movement

.   .   .   .   .

Aging: to show signs of growing old

Process: a continuing development involving many changes

.   .   .   .   .

IF CHAPTER 3 MADE the case that older adulthood is a period of growth and development by adding two developmental stages to Erik Erikson's life-cycle theory, this chapter will support this view by proposing that the aging process is one of forward movement. I will be making particular use in this chapter of Paul W. Pruyser's article titled "Aging: Downward, Upward, or Forward?"[1] In this article he argues against the popular view that older adulthood is a downward slide from the peak that one experiences and realizes in middle adulthood. Rather, like the previous periods in one's life, older adulthood should be viewed as one of forward movement.

As we will see, Pruyser is especially interested in the losses and gains experienced in the process of growing older, and he views the losses as well as the gains as playing a very significant role in one's ongoing growth and development. Moreover, the idea that the aging process is one of

1. Pruyser, "Aging"

forward movement invites us to think of it as a journey, one that necessarily includes detours and backward steps. While these detours and
backward steps may appear to be counterproductive, I believe that they
more typically contribute to one's growth and ongoing development.

As we will be focusing on essays by Paul W. Pruyser in this and the
following chapter, readers may like to know a bit about him: Born and
raised in the Netherlands, Pruyser did graduate work in psychology at
the University of Amsterdam, and emigrated to the United States in 1948
(he was thirty-two years old at the time) and completed his doctoral work
in clinical psychology at Boston University in 1953. He spent virtually all
his professional career at the Menninger Foundation in Topeka, Kansas,
where he was director of the Department of Education from 1962 to 1971
and Professor of Research and Education in Psychiatry until his retirement in 1985. He was editor of the *Bulletin of the Menninger Foundation*
until his death in 1987.[2]

The Downward-Slide Conception of Older Adulthood

Pruyser begins his article titled "Aging: Downward, Upward, or Forward?" with a critique of the prevailing view of older adulthood as a
downward slide from the peak of middle adulthood. He notes that although "it is true that views on aging vary with culture and change with
the times, nearly all Western views of aging are similar in one respect,"
namely, "the overruling conviction that life has a peak, somewhere, with
an upward and a downward slope on either side."[3] He quotes the first four
lines from a sonnet by William Shakespeare as a poetical expression of
this conviction:

> When forty winters shall besiege thy brow
> And dig deep trenches in thy beauty's field,
> The youth's proud livery, so gazed on now,
> Will be a tatter'd weed, of small worth held.[4]

---

2. His books include *A Dynamic Psychology of Religion, Between Belief and Unbelief, The Minister as Diagnostician,* and *The Play of the Imagination.*

3. Pruyser, "Aging," 102.

4. Shakespeare, *The Complete Works,* 1595. Like most sonnets, this one does not
simply continue in the same vein for another ten lines but instead begins at line nine
(the traditional turning shift) to suggest that the loss of one's physical beauty is com-
pensated for if one has been the parent of a "fair child." This shift in perspective does

He adds, "It does not matter greatly whether the peak is at thirty, forty, or fifty years" as these differences "may depend on the average expectable life span, the composition of the population pyramid, the epidemiology of illness, the economic system, and the education and welfare policies of a society."[5] What does matter is that the "visual imagination sees a peak, flanked by valleys, one rising, one declining, in an aesthetically satisfying symmetry."[6] Thus, "life views are shaped by a regnant Gestalt of low-high-low proportions, an iconic illusion that pre-sorts all perceptions of the life cycle into a triphasic sequence."[7]

Pruyser points out that there are an infinite number of representations of this "iconic illusion," and that each one of them reinforces the basic idea so strongly that we take the illusion for reality "until a rare or unexpected occasion elicits some puzzlement."[8] In addition to the *literary* form of which Shakespeare's sonnet is only one example, these representations include the *symmetrical* model of the peak flanked by two valleys; the *curve* model used in empirical research, with its elevated middle section tapering off evenly on either side; the *linear* model which presents the image of the arc of life with its summit in the middle; the *existential* version as a stretch of contingency, arched in the middle, suspended between the "thrownness" of birth and "pushed-outness" of death; the *journeyer's* model depicting a crawling babe rising to become a walking, erect adult who in turn becomes a shuffling, cane-supported oldster; the *activity* model which puts work in the middle, preceded by play, and followed by retirement (perhaps another word for *play*); and the *economic* model which centers on the productive years in the middle preceded by a vague stretch of teenage consumerism and followed by the "golden years" of eroding capital.[9]

Pruyser also notes that this *iconic illusion* is found in the *arts* where it is "reinforced by the triptychs of church altars with their major center

---

not directly challenge Pruyser's view that the poem reflects the "overruling conviction" that life has a peak and that those beyond a certain age (here forty years old) are on a downward slope. At the same time, its mention of a compensating factor supports Pruyser's view, presented later in the article, that old age is not only one of loss but also one of newly experienced gains.

5. Pruyser, "Aging," 102.

6. Ibid., 102.

7. Ibid., 102–3.

8. Ibid., 103.

9. Ibid.

panels and minor side wings" and "by the cascading structure of great churches and palaces whose major cupolas and spires are centered to draw one's gaze to a rise, peak, and fall pattern."[10] As these artistic forms of the iconic illusion involve church architecture they have powerful religious or spiritual support as well. But if this iconic illusion is found in great churches and palaces, "its *homeliest* form is probably the Victorian fireplace mantel arrangement whose centerpiece, the clock, is flanked by two ornamental vases that are kept completely dysfunctional." In short, "so much in the world proclaims a tripartite or triphasic pattern with a dominant center that we come to think of this pattern as a cosmic, ordained reality, and as a leitmotiv of life," and given its ubiquity, "this powerful iconic illusion thwarts us from seeing, or making, alternative patterns."[11]

On the other hand, there are visions of aging that differ from this rise, peak, and fall pattern. For example, the Greeks prized youth and old age but seemed to find little to admire about the middle years. Also, in some societies, especially those with established patterns of ancestor worship, "the aged have such venerable status and benefits that aging is a positive goal of life and a desirable process."[12] At the other extreme, there are societies in which "older people have not only been denigrated, as they are by and large today, but were even sent into the wilderness to die."[13]

Pruyser notes that these various models indicate "that culture is a powerful determinant of attitudes toward aging and, hence, of feelings about selfhood at any age of life."[14] In fact, "the impact of cultural factors on aging is so strong that it is foolish to belittle them as less real than the biology of aging." Also, although cultural factors are in principle more changeable than biological factors, cultural change does not come easily, so if we want our conceptions about aging to change, we need to supplement "scientific data-gathering" with "existential inquiries and con-

---

10. Ibid.

11. Ibid.

12. Ibid., 104.

13. Ibid. It may be that the venerable status accorded the old in some societies is not all that different from the denigration they receive in other societies. For veneration may have the subtle or not so subtle implication of the venerated person's irrelevance in society. This may also apply, at least to some extent, to attributions of wisdom to the older adult.

14. Ibid., 104.

sciousness-raising, with keen alertness to the ideological consequences that follow from the dominant iconic illusion of aging."[15]

Unfortunately, it is very difficult to find even provisional agreement on what aging is. If aging is *growing*, in what sense does growing continue, stop, or change with the years? If aging is *coming of age*, time markers are introduced that set off one period of life from another for reasons of privilege and duty. If aging is *maturing*, the noun *maturity* introduces normative ideas about the course of the process denoted by the verb, and these ideas are then elaborated by notions of ripeness, overripeness, and rottenness borrowed from horticulture. If aging is *getting on in years*, we may think of judgment beginning to prevail over action and also of a sense of fatigue or even of vulnerability and depression. If aging is taken as the process meant to eventuate in *being aged*, it is largely seen as a foreboding of failing powers and eventual death.[16]

Pruyser observes that in the light of these variations in outlook and meaning the so-called facts of aging have a rather dubious status, for many of these are functions of particular viewpoints, disciplines, and social and personal observations. Moreover, the few facts that we do have are so minute and piecemeal that their significance is unclear, as there is no way of assigning specific weight to them. For example, autopsies have shown gross erosion of an entire brain hemisphere in older persons who nonetheless experienced exemplary physical and mental preservation until their last days. How can we weigh this fact against, for example, the slowing of reaction times in reflexes over time?

In light of these difficulties of fact-finding and knowing what to make of the few facts that *are* available, it would be easy to become nihilistic about the very idea that we can gain some understanding of the aging process. But for Pruyser, such nihilism is unwarranted, because we *do* know a few things about the aging process. One is that there is no escape from what St. Augustine identifies as the three presents—a present of things past, of things present, and things future—and the fact that they "gradually assume different ratios in each person's life."[17] Nor can one overlook the fact that there is a "waning of physical vigor and alacrity of

15. Ibid., 104.
16. Ibid., 104–5.
17. Ibid., 105.

mind as the years roll by," and that death "lurks around the corner and can be held at bay for only so long."[18]

Pruyser suggests that "the vital balance" of the life process quivers precariously between the two forces of life and death—with death having the edge in the long run by the sheer weight of its inertia—and that our increasing awareness of this eventual inertia and of the feelings it engenders is central to our basic understanding of the aging process. He adds that we experience this "vital balance" of the life process as "an ongoing process of losses and gains, mourning and rejoicing."[19] Unfortunately, we "know quite a bit about the losses, and very little about the gains," and this is largely "because aging has so often been described, under the aegis of our iconic illusion, as a stepwise approach to decrepitude."[20] To address this imbalance, Pruyser devotes the remaining pages of the article to the task of identifying the losses and the gains that accompany the aging process.

Losses in the Aging Process

Although the losses that accompany the aging process have been discussed far more than the gains, Pruyser cautions that we should not for this reason "deny or play down these losses, for coping with them is one of the taxing and energy-consuming features of aging," and having to cope with them may "accelerate the aging process and set up spiral effects."[21] Moreover, "failure in coping with any specific loss undermines the aptness of one's response to the next loss, while success in coping with one loss may give one the vigor to face the next with bravery and skill."[22]

His discussion of these losses focuses on those that especially involve "personal setbacks." The first such "personal setback" is *the loss of personal dignity.* Older adults "are subject to many indignities that are experienced as a frontal attack on their self-concept, their feeling of self-worth, and the maintenance mechanisms of self-regard."[23] Also, it makes

---

18. Ibid.

19. Ibid., 105. *The Vital Balance* is the title of a book written by Karl Menninger with the assistance of Martin Mayman and Paul W. Pruyser.

20. Ibid., 107.

21. Ibid.

22. Ibid.

23. Ibid. 108.

very little difference whether these assaults on one's dignity are purely societal, or whether they are enhanced or perpetuated by the victims themselves through attitudes of self-fulfilling prophecy; for, regardless, the experience is felt as a narcissistic blow. Since these blows may be harder today and be felt by more people than in former ages due to the increase in average life-span expectancy, an irony of this increase in average life-span expectancy is that more people are exposed to the indignities of old age.

The second personal setback is the *loss of work*, a loss that "runs a close second in importance to loss of dignity, and may be intimately linked with it."[24] Pruyser cites a book by Studs Terkel on the work of ordinary or low-income people that shows that "workers, by and large, tend to endow their jobs with a profound sense of vocation full of humanistic, religious, or ethical values that make them feel a significant part of a quasi-sacred scheme, even if they are by social standards no more than cogs in a machine."[25] Pruyser suggests that these attitudes toward work "seem to capture some meanings of the theological concept of vocation or calling, in which work (of any sort) makes one a participant in creation and providence, giving each person a definite place and a significant role in a cosmic plan." In this sense, the loss of work is the loss of vocation, "depriving a person of the concrete experience of values and meaning."[26]

Work also provides a framework for reality testing and this is a very important factor in mental health: "Work brings a person into forced contact with the nature of things and materials, with the resistance of matter, with the contours and definitions of ideas, and the nature of cause and effect relations, with sensory qualities, mass and force."[27] Thus, work "draws us out of ourselves into the world; it forces us to deal with the actual outlines of reality, shoulders us with obligations, and harnesses our energies."[28] Also, given the importance of the sense of time to our perception of the aging process, work is valuable because it "structures the flow of time for us into distinct periods for action and relaxation, work and play." Similarly, it structures space "by giving us opportunities to talk about our work while we are at home and to talk about home when

24. Ibid., 108.

25. Ibid. Terkel's book is titled *Working: People Talk about What They Do All Day and How They Feel about What They Do*.

26. Pruyser, "Aging," 108.

27. Ibid., 108.

28. Ibid., 109.

we are at work." Thus, the loss of work "demolishes this outer structuring device and forces us to impose arrangements on time and space and social intercourse that have to be created de novo by what inner structuring resources we have."[29]

A third significant personal loss is the *loss of independence.* Pruyser notes that dependency and independence are relative ideas and perceptions, yet they act as a value orientation because our development requires that we move in one direction from a state of dependency in childhood to one of independence in adulthood. He adds that "in our culture we are exhorted to be maximally independent." In fact, the very

> ideal of maturity prescribes self-sufficiency, self-help, competence in managing one's own affairs, a display of unshakable strength in the face of adversity, the ability to seek and organize one's own pleasures and to ward off pain effectively, skill in seeking our own sources of contact and support, capacity for making friends, ability to earn one's own money, and strength to be a good spouse or parent or a satisfied single adult.[30]

Thus, independence is viewed as a critical component of the capacity to connect with and relate meaningfully to others.

If independence is the maturational and cultural goal, it can be very upsetting when events in the life cycle force us to surrender it, bit by bit, and "the upset is even worse when one incisive event, such as retirement, produces many losses at once."[31] It is also understandable that any new dependency "is feared as an insult, evaluated as a regression, and experienced as loss of a once-prized achievement!"[32] Pruyser cites here the decline in income at retirement, auditory and visual losses, and dependence on "gadgets and aids, pills and rest periods, memory props, and special transportation arrangements."[33]

A fourth personal setback is the *loss of time,* especially in the sense that one is running out of available time:

> Reality testing suggests that with more personal time behind one, there is less time ahead. The future is no longer a virtually endless stretch. And there is still so much to do, there are so

29. Ibid.
30. Ibid.
31. Ibid.
32. Ibid.
33. Ibid., 109–10.

many projects to start or finish, so many longings that should
be fulfilled.[34]

In addition, there are those who feel that "so many repairs must still be
made of things done poorly in the past, so many faults to be set straight,
so much atonement to be undertaken for previous transgressions."[35]

Little wonder, then, that the very feeling that one is aging tends to
promote a degree of agitation, restlessness, or hurry. To be sure, these
feelings are found among persons in midlife too, but there tends to be
a greater sense of urgency in the later years. Also, although exemption
from work "puts much new chronological time at a person's disposal," one
"may not know at all what to do with this time; it is unstructured." Hence
the conundrum of "too little time on the one hand, too much on the other
hand; too little for personal synthesis and further maturation, too much
for dreaming, trifles, and busywork." Such "situational ambiguity" may,
in turn, "activate all kinds of personal ambivalence," thus increasing the
agitation and making "the task of coping all the more strenuous."[36]

Finally, Pruyser adds to these four experiences of loss "a more basic
meaning of loss to which these particular losses owe much of their pain,"
namely, the *loss of object relations*. The essence of *object relations* for his
purposes here is that "selfhood is a developmental and dynamic function
of our relations to other persons, and vice versa."[37] Our nascent selves
"emerge from loyalties we have toward others, and the love of others is
co-determined by the love we have of ourselves," and this means that even
as "every gain in loving, being loved, and being lovable is satisfying and
joyful," so "every loss is frustrating, saddening, and anger-provoking."
There is also the fact that the very things we value—such as money, independence, success, competence, productivity, dignity, strength, fertility,
a healthy and reliable body—are "taken as proofs of our lovability when
they come our way" and are "intertwined with our love for the significant
persons in our lives who modeled them as virtues." Thus, the loss of these
things we value creates a sense that "we are no longer loved as we were
before and can no longer love in return as before." Worse yet, these losses
"may not only be taken as signs of rejection but also become charged with

34. Ibid., 110.
35. Ibid.
36. Ibid.
37. Ibid.

irrational feelings of guilt and shame, which may turn them into punishment for transgressions or proofs of our disloyalties."[38]

Pruyser concludes his discussion of the losses sustained in the later stages of the aging process with the observation that older persons, especially the very old, are prone to experience any or all of these losses as *abandonment*. He explains:

> Being seen and heard in the marketplaces of life depends to a large extent on one's own initiative, drive, and agility; if any of these functions diminish, as they do in aging, through sensory and motor deficiencies and depletion of energy, one is simply less seen and heard.[39]

Others may make helpful efforts to give the older person a forum, but such extra efforts by others are rather infrequent, whether from forgetfulness or malignant rejection.[40] In any event, "the aged person may well feel abandoned," and this feeling of abandonment may "re-enliven old childhood memories of abandonment and mourning" and be experienced as the precursor to "the ultimate abandonment of death."[41]

When we consider these losses in light of Pruyser's earlier discussion of the "iconic illusion" and other ways of conceptualizing the life process, we can readily see that these losses are largely responsible for the very fact that the life process is referred to as an *aging* process. From time to time, Pruyser speaks of the *maturational* process, but when he does so, he typically contrasts it with the *aging* process, which seems to have a more negative connotation. Thus, although he is critical of the iconic illusion of life that posits a peak in middle adulthood followed by a decline in late adulthood, the very use of the word *aging* to describe the life process suggests that the later years are not as satisfactory as the earlier years. And, of course, his identification of the losses that occur in older adulthood reinforces this suggestion.

However, I am more concerned here with the fact that Pruyser views the life process as a forward movement. It is not, as the iconic illusion imagines it, a peak with a preceding upward slope and a succeeding

38. Ibid., 111.

39. Ibid.

40. The very fact that these thoughtful gestures are viewed as "extra effort" may also suggest that one is being patronized, as needing special assistance or treatment because one is presumed to be incapable of doing what one formerly did with relative ease.

41. Pruyser, "Aging," 111.

downward slope but a forward movement on a level plane. It is significant, therefore, that he refers to the losses sustained in older adulthood
as "personal setbacks," for the very word *setback* has the connotation of
"a reversal" or an "interruption in progress."[42] Thus, setbacks are an impediment to one's forward movement. It is also noteworthy that in his
descriptions of individual losses Pruyser uses the words "progression"
and "regression" to express the idea that in older adulthood one continues to move forward but also experiences backward tendencies that are
generally negative and to be avoided if possible. On the other hand, he
suggests that a loss may "accelerate the aging process," thus implying that
the forward movement may be faster than it ought to be. And, finally,
he notes that, in older adulthood, the forward movement we experience
in life is no longer perceived as a "virtually endless stretch." Instead, it is
viewed as limited in time or duration. Moreover, it terminates in death.[43]

Thus, we have reason to raise questions regarding the very use of
the language of progression for forward movement and regression for
backward movement, especially if death is not viewed as a desirable goal,
end point, or terminus of the aging process. While some older adults
welcome or even long for death, most prefer that life will go on, even if
this means having to cope with the losses that Pruyser identifies here. In
either case, the losses that occur in older adulthood indicate that the view
of life as forward movement has some intriguing ironies and paradoxes.
In order to see these in perspective, we need to consider his discussion of
the potential gains in the aging process.

Potential Gains in Aging

Pruyser anticipates the foregoing comments on the ironies and paradoxes
raised by his proposal that the life process is one of forward movement by
beginning his discussion of the "potential gains in aging" with the observation that up to this point he seems "to have only reinforced the iconic
illusion of a low-high-low sequential pattern."[44] He agrees that this is, in
fact, the case, for much as he "struggled to extricate myself from it, I have
demonstrated how much I am still its captive." But now he wants to liber-

42. Agnes et al., eds., *Webster's New World College Dictionary*, 1312.

43. The belief in a personal afterlife is not based on the view that this afterlife is
integral to the aging process; rather, it is a new beginning or rebirth.

44. Pruyser, "Aging," 111.

ate himself, as it were, by asking readers at this juncture "to consider the fact that many aging persons seem to take their successive losses rather well and do not succumb prematurely to the strains of aging."[45] He asks, "Do they have exceptional coping skills, or does the aging process itself bestow gains and compensations for the losses it imposes?"[46] Pruyser believes that much is to be said for the latter explanation; for the very fact that many individuals—not just the "happy few"—appear to age with "a good deal of tranquility and considerable happiness" suggests that they are "making some psychic gains and experiencing some satisfactions along with the losses they sustain."[47]

One such gain is *the gradual discovery of some good and wholesome adult dependencies.* Pruyser explains, "When the children have grown up, the parents begin to see how much they depend on their children's liveliness, attestations of love and goodwill, and their presence as objects of caring."[48] Sometimes this realization is a reaction to the "empty nest" syndrome as spouses, "after having taken each other for granted, discover how much they need one another." Also, the necessity of planning for retirement may result in the discovery of how much we have depended on our regular work for daily satisfactions and mental equilibrium, and we may begin to take a new look at our former strivings for independence, finding some of it suspect: "By hindsight, some of it was very demanding and overdone, and the promoted ideal of independence now proves to have been rather fictitious." With this realization, one may begin to relax and to acknowledge "the healthiness of some dependencies" and to entertain the thought that "some specific dependencies (e.g., on one's children, pension plans, friendships, recreation, simpler housing, mass transportation) are likely to increase with the years."[49]

A second gain is the satisfaction that results from *redefining one's own status.* Formerly defined by occupation, income, and social approval of one's demonstrated zeal for "making it" (all of which are external status definitions), "the status of the person who knows that he is aging becomes increasingly defined by himself, in terms of his personal criteria."[50] The

45. Ibid.
46. Ibid., 111–12.
47. Ibid., 112.
48. Ibid.
49. Ibid.
50. Ibid.

achievement motive and the social approval one receives for it may give way to a search for personal satisfactions, and whatever forms this may take, we find a new niche for ourselves that tallies with our native bent and preferences rather than with the dictates of upward mobility and pressures for conformity. Thus, "fateful as aging may be in many ways, it also gives new margins of independence for taking a greater hand in shaping one's own role and status."[51]

A third potential gain, one that often builds on the second, derives from the fact that aging affords the *opportunity for discovering one's own inner world as a worthy complement of, or alternative to, the external world to which one has been enslaved for so long*: "With a good deal of experience and many memories to look back on, one is in a position to take stock of oneself," and especially to discover that much of the self was thwarted by undue attention to the "masked" self of social expectation, and that "keen strivings for action" had cut oneself off from "the satisfactions of contemplation."[52] In turn, these self-discoveries may enable one to develop new ways of relating to the external world, to embrace "an ever wider circle of humanity with whom one can identify without pointed personal or parental narcissism."[53] One may befriend whomever one chooses to befriend, to enjoy encounters with a great variety of people from all walks of life, and become "less afraid of slurs of eccentricity."[54]

A fourth potential gain is the *relaxing of defenses*. With greater and more profound knowledge of the inevitable ambiguities of life and an acceptance of the ambivalences of one's own feelings, unpleasant realities can be faced with less denial. Moreover, when the hypervigilance promoted by the rat-race image of life calms down to normal alertness, and the need to create and maintain defenses begins to diminish, one's energies can be put to better use. To put these freed-up energies to better use, some older persons seek or create work. This *may* in some instances be "a defensive maneuver against the imminence of death," as a means either to avoid thinking about death or to consign it to a distant future date because there is so much that needs to be accomplished in the meantime. But, in Pruyser's view, it is likely to be much more than that, for "work structures time and space, as well as personality," and "some work produces gifts

---

51. Ibid.
52. Ibid., 113.
53. Ibid.
54. Ibid., 114.

that convey love symbolically," such as things that grandparents make for their children and grandchildren.[55]

A fifth potential gain is a newly discovered capacity to *live in the present*. If in earlier stages of life one was "rushing toward the future with feverish expectations and deep worries," older persons often "enjoy more because what they enjoy is now, in the present moment."[56] These pleasures may be small and unspectacular, but they are real. In the case of religious individuals, "the faith that sustained them in dark moments of the past, perhaps defensively, is now an enjoyable cosmology that beautifies and validates their present days."[57]

This allusion to religious faith in the context of a discussion of the older person's capacity to live in the present prompts Pruyser to comment briefly on two related issues. The first concerns the fact that persons in the later stages of life tend to think more than they did previously about their own "approximate life span." Some believe on the basis of intuition or family statistics that their life span will be longer rather than shorter. Others, on the same basis, anticipate otherwise. In either case,

> The older one gets, the closer one moves into having to come to terms with dying. In his early fifties, Freud wrote in a letter to Jung: "Old age is not an empty delusion." There are hard tasks to be done. Being very old means having to prepare oneself for death, pondering its meaning, or seeking a meaningful relation to its closeness. Faith, hope, love and their permutations in all kinds of philosophies and religion are now put into the crucible—one becomes a kind of solitary alchemist doing his last "crucial" experiments.[58]

The second issue concerns developmental psychology and, more specifically, the contrast between the minute, age-specific groups into which the young have been subdivided and the tendency to lump older adults together into a single age group "as though they formed one homogeneous mass."[59] Pruyser notes:

> The category of "the aged" may span as many as four or five whole decades! Despite efforts at conceiving some subdivision,

55. Ibid.
56. Ibid.
57. Ibid., 114–15.
58. Ibid, 115.
59. Ibid.

I am not sure that any compelling developmental distinctions have yet been made with a holistic tenor; most of them are of situational, fiscal, medical, or physiological orientation, or based on rather arbitrary chronological age brackets. We really do not yet know what the feasible distinctions are because we have been ideologically so resistant to investigating the process of aging.[60]

Since Pruyser may well have had Erikson's life-cycle model in mind when he observed that developmental theories lump older adults together into one age group, it would be interesting to know whether he would have endorsed the proposal presented in chapter 3. Although he says that we do not know enough to make the sorts of distinctions that such proposals make, it is worth noting that he uses decade language in his suggestion that such distinctions would be helpful.

A sixth potential gain is the aging person's *capacity to make identifications or re-identifications with the idealism of youth and to take vicarious pleasure in young persons' activism.* Pruyser suggests that a generational factor may be operating here:

Skipping the intervening generation with its dedication to thought control and behavior shaping and its penchant for judging and disciplining, aging persons often feel attracted to youth and deal with young people in a relaxed way, tolerant of their foibles and positively charmed by their idealism and venturesomeness.[61]

Conversely, "many young people feel attracted to the aged, finding them surprisingly congenial and avant-garde in comparison with the generation of their parents."[62] Pruyser notes that delight in one's own grandchildren "partakes of these qualities," but he believes that the older person's identification with the idealism of youth transcends narrowly defined family associations and loyalties; that, in fact, "the rediscovery of youth and its goodness amounts to a carefree caring that stands in contrast to the anxious (and more narcissistic) caring that prevailed during the years of parental responsibility."[63]

60. Ibid.

61. Ibid. The older person's identification with the idealism of youth may also be an expression, as discussed in chapter 2, of one's desire to reconnect with the youth who continues to live inside oneself.

62. Ibid., 115.

63. Ibid., 116.

A seventh potential gain is that aging gives *a new freedom for reveal-ing one's innermost thoughts.* Pruyser believes that this freedom "pertains to many ordinary people and is not confined to luminaries" who, in their advanced years, share their personal credos with the public. He describes this new freedom:

> However honest and open a person may have been before, ag-ing gives him a new candor for speaking without inhibitions. He reaps the satisfactions of a delayed honesty and a latter day openness that exceed everything he has been before. He has less fear of mockery and retaliation; he can now emotionally afford to show his heart in his reasoning.[64]

For some, this freer spirit leads to "an appropriate militancy in secur-ing one's rights, or in doing battle for any oppressed part of humanity."[65] Among the examples he cites, he mentions Karl Menninger's activism for prison reform in his later years.

Pruyser concludes that if these peculiar gains of aging are taken into account, and without denying that losses also occur, "life seems no longer to fit the iconic illusion of the low-high-low sequence."[66] Rather, "a new image shapes up." Recalling the *homeliest* artistic form of the iconic illu-sion, "it is as if someone put a bouquet of flowers in the right hand vase that stands on the Victorian mantelpiece." This bouquet of flowers "has the power to distract our gaze from the dominance of the clock in the middle."[67]

Detours and Backward Steps

In the concluding sentence of the abstract of his article, Pruyser states: "Aging's gains and losses are described, leading to the conclusion that the life course is neither upward nor downward, but a forward movement full of new discoveries."[68] In my view, he has made a persuasive case for the conclusion that the life course is neither an upward nor downward movement but a forward movement. Yet, as we have also seen, he refers to the losses sustained in older adulthood as "personal setbacks," thus

64. Ibid.
65. Ibid.
66. Ibid., 117.
67. Ibid.
68. Ibid. 102.

suggesting that they can be an impediment to one's forward movement; and in his descriptions of individual losses he uses the words "progression" and "regression" to express the idea that in older adulthood one continues to move forward but also experiences backward tendencies that are generally negative and to be avoided if possible. On the other hand, a loss may "accelerate the aging process," which suggests that the forward movement is faster than it ought to be.

Thus, as I noted in our consideration of the losses that occur in older adulthood, there are various ironies and paradoxes in the very fact that the aging process is one of forward movement. I would now like to expand on this point by returning to the discussion in chapter 3 of Freud's idea of the death instinct. As we will see, Freud's views on the death instinct and its interaction with the life instincts draw attention to the detours and backward steps that occur in the aging process.

To initiate this reconsideration of Freud's views on the death instinct, I suggest that we revisit Pruyser's observation, early in his article, that "the vital balance" of the life process "quivers between the two forces of life and death, always precariously," and that "death has the edge in the long run by the sheer weight of its inertia."[69] Here, Pruyser is invoking Freud's views on the life and death instincts and making an association between these views and Karl Menninger's book *The Vital Balance,* to which Pruyser himself contributed.

In his study of the Menninger family and the clinic that they founded, Lawrence J. Friedman discusses the role that Freud's theory of the death instinct played in Karl Menninger's development of his concept of "the vital balance."[70] Friedman notes that Menninger's earlier books, *Man against Himself* and *Love against Hate,* were based on Freud's theory of the death instinct,[71] and that by "developing Freud's concept of a deep, powerful force of *thanatos* (the death instinct) emerging and contesting *eros* (the life instinct) within a person, Karl sought to outline in these volumes what he regarded as Freud's most important message—man's tragic intrapsychic struggle."[72]

On the other hand, Friedman points out that in both books Menninger "treated the death instinct as a less ominous force than Freud had

69. Ibid., 105.

70. Friedman, *Menninger,* 120–25.

71. Menninger, *Man against Himself;* Menninger, *Love against Hate.*

72. Friedman, *Menninger,* 120.

given his followers to believe," that he not only "claimed that its manifestations were detectable in a clinical examination" but also "character-
ized it as an eminently manageable phenomenon."[73] This is not to say
that these were "distortions or popularizations" of Freud's dual-instinct
theory. Rather, they reflected the fact that in certain areas, Menninger
"openly and thoughtfully departed from key Freudian tenets."[74] For example, in *Man against Himself* he argued that within each person there
is an equilibrium between *eros* and *thanatos*, and that it is often unstable.
Thus, in contrast to Freud's view of *eros* and *thanatos* as absolute qualities,
Menninger saw them as the two polar extremes on a continuum. In this
way, the clash between the two instincts "was reformulated so that the
focus was no longer on either of the polar extremities but on how and
why a person moved from one pole to another."[75] Friedman indicates that
Menninger's *The Vital Balance* is his clearest presentation of his concept
of shifts on a continuum between *eros* and *thanatos*.

As we saw in chapter 3, Freud introduced his theory of the death
instinct in *Beyond the Pleasure Principle* in his discussion of the compulsion to repeat (or the repetition compulsion). He notes that this compulsion is especially found among children. With adults a joke produces
almost no effect when heard for a second time, and it is hard to persuade
someone who enjoyed reading a book to reread it immediately. Not so
with children. They "will never tire of asking an adult to repeat a game
that he has shown them or played with them," and "if a child has been
told a nice story, he will insist on hearing it over and over again rather
than a new one." He will also insist that the repetition is "an identical one
and will correct any alterations of which the narrator may be guilty."[76]
Freud contends that this difference between adults and children is due to
the fact that the children's behavior is more deeply instinctual than that of
the adult. If so, this means that the compulsion to repeat is a manifestation "of a universal attribute of instincts and perhaps of organic life in
general which has not hitherto been clearly recognized or at least not
explicitly stressed." Thus,

> *It seems, then, that an instinct is an urge inherent in organic life to
> restore an earlier state of things* which the living entity has been

73. Ibid., 121.

74. Ibid.

75. Ibid., 124.

76. Freud, *Beyond the Pleasure Principle,* 66.

obliged to abandon under the pressure of external disturbing forces; that is, it is a kind of organic elasticity, or, to put it another way, the expression of an inertia inherent in organic life.[77]

Freud goes on to note that if there is an urge inherent in organic life to restore an earlier state of things, then it would contradict the conservative nature of the instincts if the goal of life were a state of things that had never yet been attained. Rather, the goal of life would need to be "an *old* state of things, an initial state from which the living entity has at one time or other departed by the circuitous paths along which its development leads."[78] Furthermore, if we accept the view that "everything living dies for *internal* reasons—becomes inorganic once again—then we shall be compelled to say that '*the aim of all life is death*' and, looking backwards, that '*inanimate things existed before living ones*.'"[79]

If, however, there was a time when all that existed was inanimate matter, then at some point "a force of whose nature we can form no conception" evoked the "attributes of life" in inanimate matter. This created a "tension" in the living being between its animate state and its inanimate state, and this tension resulted in the first instinct coming into being, "the instinct to return to the inanimate state."[80] Initially, it was still an easy matter for a living substance to die, but as time went on, "decisive external influences altered in such a way as to oblige the still surviving substance to diverge ever more widely from its original course of life and to make ever more complicated *detours* before reaching its aim of death." Freud concludes: "These circuitous paths to death, faithfully kept to by the conservative instincts, would thus present us with the picture of the phenomena of life."[81]

Most critical commentary on Freud's death instinct has focused on the question of whether the organism does, in fact, have an instinctual

77. Ibid., 67 (italics original).

78. Ibid., 70.

79. Ibid., 70–71 (italics original).

80. Ibid., 71. Freud is aware that this "force," which evoked the attributes of life in inanimate matter, has been conceptualized in the world's religions and in philosophical and literary writings. Given his Jewish heritage, he would have been very familiar with the account in Genesis 1–2 of God's creation of an animate world, which included breathing into the nostrils of man the breath of life. Given his awareness of this and other conceptualizations, we may conclude that he is speaking for himself when he says that the nature of this force is inconceivable (i.e., that what this force was is impossible to identify or name, much less describe).

81. Ibid., 71.

aim toward death. Little has been written about Freud's idea that as time went on, external influences led to the development of various detours and setbacks on the road to death, thus making this road more circuitous. The dictionary defines *detour* as "a roundabout way; deviation from a direct way" and as "a route used when the direct or regular route is closed to traffic."[82] Thus, a *detour* is an impediment to forward movement toward our destination. Some *detours* are rather inconsequential as they may only involve going a few blocks out of our way. Others are more significant, taking us several miles in another direction before reconnecting with the highway or road on which we were originally traveling. In these cases we may "lose" a substantial amount of time, which, in turn, may cause us to arrive much later at our destination than we originally planned. As a result, *detours* can be frustrating, and in some cases they can have serious consequences, as when an ambulance transporting a desperately ill person to a hospital encounters a major *detour*.

If, however, the destination is death or the return of the living organism to its inanimate state, we are likely to view *detours* quite differently. Freud suggests that when the instinct to return to the inanimate state first came into existence, it was still an easy matter "for a living substance to die," for "the course of its life was probably only a brief one," its direction being determined "by the chemical structure of the young life."[83] When this way of looking at things is applied to the human organism, we are likely to view *detours* as a godsend, and may even think of God not only as the force that evoked the attributes of life in inanimate matter (the original creative act) but also as the primary "external circumstance" that implanted in our progenitors the very disposition toward *detours*, thus endowing the human species with its own creative capacities.

In addition to *detours,* Freud suggests that the organism may take *backward steps* that have the effect of prolonging its journey on the road to death. This suggestion occurs in a discussion of the sexual instincts. Invoking his earlier observation that external circumstances have played an important role in causing the organism to diverge from its path toward its original inanimate state, Freud notes that some organisms have successfully resisted these external pressures and as a result have remained up to the present time at their original, uncomplicated level. But other organisms have developed internal features (he refers to them

82. Agnes et al., eds., *Webster's New World College Dictionary,* 393.
83. Freud, *Beyond the Pleasure Principle,* 71.

as germ-cells) that, over time, have taken on a life of their own, separate from the organism as a whole. These germ-cells "work against the death of the living substance and succeed in winning for it what we can only regard as potential immortality, though that may mean no more than a lengthening of the road to death."[84]

Freud suggests that these germ-cells would not be able to work against the death of the living substance if they were not supported by instincts no less conservative than the death instinct, but in a very different way—for these instincts seek to bring the organism back "to earlier states of *living* substance."[85] Thus, they are conservative not only in the sense that they are "peculiarly resistant to external influences" but also in the sense that "they preserve life itself for a comparatively long period." These are "the true life instincts," and they "operate against the purpose of the other instincts, which leads, by reason of their function, to death." As a result, the life of the organism moves with "a vacillating rhythm": "One group of instincts rushes forward so as to reach the final aim of life as swiftly as possible; but when a particular stage in the advance has been reached, *the other group jerks back to a certain point to make a fresh start and so prolong the journey.*"[86]

Here, Freud contends that there are *internal* instincts that arrest the organism's movement toward its final destination, which is death, and that they accomplish this by a backward movement that produces a fresh start and thereby prolongs the journey. This is not a detour due to external circumstances but a backward thrust under the aegis of internal instincts—instincts whose aim is not death but life. Freud's use of the word *prolong* is especially noteworthy because it means "to lengthen or extend in time or space."[87] The journey is prolonged because one retraces one's steps to an earlier spot or place and then retraces them again as one continues forward. Thus, the "jerking back" means that this part of the journey will not only be repeated, but that it will take twice as long

84. Ibid, 74. Menninger is critical of Freud's adoption of the germ-cell theory formulated by A. Weissman, because it is based on the fallacious idea that the organism was originally "dust" and that when it dies it "returns to dust." See Menninger, *The Vital Balance,* 117. But perhaps Freud's attraction to this theory was due in part to its association to the idea expressed in Gen 3:19: that "you are dust, and to dust you shall return" (NRSV).

85. Freud, *Beyond the Pleasure Principle,* 74 (italics added).

86. Ibid., 74–75 (italics added).

87. Agnes et al., eds., *Webster's New World College Dictionary,* 1148.

as it did originally. If the end point of the journey is death, then this prolonging of the journey delays death. While it is true that we cannot "cheat" death of its eventual victory, we can delay it by taking a step back to prolong the journey.

This brings us back to our earlier discussion of the ironies and paradoxes involved in the view of the aging process as forward movement, and, more specifically, to Pruyser's reference to the losses sustained in older adulthood as "personal setbacks." If we think of the backward step as an inhibition in the forward movement of the life process, we may reframe this *loss* as, potentially, a *gain*. We tend to think negatively about backwardness in general, and the backward step is no exception. But here the backward step is life-affirming. We might also note that although Freud suggests that the death instinct is a form of repetition because it takes the organism back to its inanimate state, the life instincts are also a form of repetition in this particular case because they repeat steps on the journey that were previously taken.

Most important, we have here the paradox that a *loss* may actually be a *gain,* and this very fact invites us to consider the possibility that the losses that Pruyser identifies in the later stages of the aging process are not necessarily negative, as they may be the very vehicles by means of which the organism prolongs the journey. To be sure, they have the appearance of being losses pure and simple, and certainly no one in his or her right mind would actively solicit them. But Pruyser suggests that the losses and gains in older adulthood often have a dialectical relationship to one another: the loss of personal dignity can lead to the relaxing of one's defenses; the loss of work can lead to the development of an expanded inner life; the loss of independence can lead to the discovery of some good and wholesome dependencies, and so forth.

Whether these loss/gain connections produce increased longevity—the literal prolongation of the journey—is not the primary issue. What ultimately matters is that the later stages of the journey reflect the fact that the aging process, which begins at birth, is *growth-oriented* from beginning to end. In this regard, it may be that it is of the very nature of older adults to be less frustrated and impatient than younger adults with the detours and backward steps on the journey of life, and more attracted to what they see along the way that, were it not for the detours and backward steps, they would not have had the opportunity, time, or freedom to notice. If, as I suggested in chapter 2, older adults have the benefit of hindsight and younger adults have the benefit of foresight, perhaps it is also true that older adults have the benefit of deeper sight (their problems with visual acuity notwithstanding), as they have the time and inclination to see what is there to see. And perhaps in this respect it is appropriate to ascribe to them, as Erikson does, the quality of wisdom.

Conclusion

Pruyser's view of the aging process as a forward movement without peaks and slopes clearly supports the view that I have emphasized in the introduction and chapter 3 that older adulthood is a period of growth and ongoing development. By invoking Freud's theory of the dual instincts, we have also been able to see that not only the gains but also the losses that occur in older adulthood may support this growth process. This is certainly not to say that the losses are insignificant and inconsequential. But perhaps it is not too much to say that the growth of older adults manifests *a vital balance* between losses and gains; and if so, then we should take particular note of the fact that the word *vital* connotes life itself.[88]

88. Ibid., 1599.

5

The Creativity of Older Adults

.   .   .   .   .

Creativity: having or showing imagination or inventiveness

.   .   .   .   .

IN THIS CHAPTER I will focus on a second article on older adulthood by Paul W. Pruyser titled "Creativity in Aging Persons."[1] He did not intend that this article would support the view that older adulthood is a time of growth and development, but we can make this connection because his view of creativity is attuned to the particular circumstances of older adulthood. In fact, there are noteworthy connections between what he writes about creativity in aging persons and the three stages of older adulthood and their psychosocial crises presented in chapter 3. For one of the ways creativity is manifest in the lives of older adults is in their ability to maintain a ratio between the positive and the negative tendency of all three psychosocial crises that favors the positive tendency.

Similarly, there are noteworthy connections between the creativity of older adults and the view presented in chapter 4 that the aging process is one of forward movement, because creativity is involved in their ability to move forward and to make positive use of necessary detours and setbacks. It could well be argued that if there is a period in one's life when

1. Pruyser, "Creativity in Aging Persons."

creativity is especially required, it is the period of older adulthood. And, as Pruyser shows, it is not only the extraordinarily gifted person who expresses and employs such creativity. In fact, the creativity of older adults is insufficiently recognized—even by older adults themselves—because it is so common and universal among older adults.

Pruyser's article titled "Creativity in Aging Persons" was published five months after his death in April 1987, at the age of seventy. Although he had retired two years earlier from his full-time position as Professor of Research and Education in Psychiatry at the Menninger Foundation, he had continued as director of the interdisciplinary-studies program, as a faculty member of the school of psychiatry and mental-health services, as a clinical consultant, and as editor of the *Bulletin of the Menninger Clinic*.

To set the stage for the discussion of this article I would like to consider briefly his earlier article "An Essay on Creativity," published in 1979.[2] I will focus specifically on his identification of three dimensions of creative persons that, in his view, are originally formed in early childhood. They are *playfulness, curiosity,* and *pleasure seeking.* While he does not refer to this discussion in his later article, I believe that it underlies much of what he has to say about the creativity of older adults.

Dimensions of Creative Persons

Pruyser begins his discussion of the dimensions of creative persons with *playfulness.* He writes, "Creativity requires both a playful attitude and skill at playing."[3] Noting that the apparent triteness of this proposition should not fool us into believing that we can dispense with it, he observes that many persons "are singularly inept at playing and are too grim or too dogmatic to assume a playful attitude."[4] This is often due to their having been deprived in childhood of opportunities to practice playing and to become skillful, and the fact that their informal education and formal instruction was boring and stiff, affording "little exposure to enticing and admirable role models."[5]

Pruyser suggests that the playful attitude and the acquisition of skill at playing "need to be buttressed by the belief that playing is more than

2. Pruyser, "An Essay on Creativity."

3. Ibid., 337.

4. Ibid.

5. Ibid., 337–38.

a diversion, that it has its own seriousness."[6] For some, its seriousness derives from the belief that one is contributing one's talents to the welfare of humanity, that one has a task to shoulder in God's creation, or that one has a responsibility to replace ugliness with beauty. But over and above these special precepts, there should be the more general belief that playing is "a quasi-sacred activity" because it puts us in touch with the mystery of our place in nature, of the human mind, and of the cosmos.[7]

The second dimension of the creative person is *curiosity*. Pruyser suggests that curiosity, as it relates to creativity, has its basis in the toddler's inquisitive preoccupation with anatomical differences and sexual acts, and therefore "involves a longing that the concealed be revealed."[8] Thus, a dialectical relationship between concealment/revelation, darkness/light, ignorance/knowing and guessing/grasping lies at the root of situations eliciting curiosity. Therefore, curiosity

> is a kind of eager search not for things that are already patently present and nameable, indeed not for things at all, but for constructions that satisfy the human thirst for order, meaning, clarity, insight, or harmony in a sensory world that is rather cluttered, in a social world that is threatening or confusing, or in a psychological world that is stormy or chaotic.[9]

The third dimension of the creative person is *pleasure seeking*. Pruyser notes that creative persons are able to connect with libidinal desires, "not only their anticipated or hoped for novelties, but also the path or instrumentation of search that may lead to a fortunate find."[10] He suggests that because the search itself is libido-laden, we should not make too sharp a distinction between preparatory and consummative acts in creative work. As examples of pleasure seeking in the creative process, Pruyser cites Pablo Picasso's "perennially lustful, twinkle-eyed, and frolicsome engagement in his visual and manual skills," and the impression one gets from listening to Johann Sebastian Bach's compositions of "joyful tonality and exuberance in 'making music,' no matter how sad the themes of some of his cantatas."[11]

6. Ibid., 338.
7. Ibid.
8. Ibid., 338–39.
9. Ibid., 339.
10. Ibid., 340.
11. Ibid., 340–41.

In addition to these three dimensions of creative persons, Pruyser discusses the role of the *release of aggression, defense dynamics,* and *adaptation* in the experience of creative persons. I will confine my comments here to adaptation, as it has particular relevance to creativity in older adulthood. Pruyser points out that as a biological term, *adaptation* concerns an organism "fitting into" the opportunities and demands of what he calls the "illusionistic world": that is, the world that exists between and beyond the inner, subjective, private world and the outer, objectively verifiable, and realistic world.[12] The illusionistic world is one in which objects assume a symbolic significance and therefore take on transcendent meaning. Pruyser calls the creative activity that occurs in the illusionistic world *illusion processing.*

There are different ways in which one may "fit into" the opportunities and demands of the illusionistic world. Some individuals are "situationally destined to specialize exhaustively in illusionistic activities and, with talent and practice, become creative." For example, they grow up in a family that values music, art, and literature. But adaptation "may also imply being at the right place at the right time in the right discipline where advances are likely or already pressing, or having a sixth sense for where the cutting edge is and grasping the chances."[13] However, the form of adaptation that concerns us here has more to do with the vicissitudes of the aging process, especially the fact that aging has effects on the human body that are undesirable. Some of these changes may not have a direct effect on the individual's creativity while others may, in which case one may abandon the activities to which one's creativity has been directed or find ways to *adapt* to the change so that one is able to continue to be creative. Such adaptation may lead to new forms or expressions of creativity, of illusion processing. If so, we can say that there is a convergence of the two forms of adaptation—biological and illusionistic—that Pruyser identifies. As we saw in the introduction, Mary Robertson Moses (known as Grandma Moses) began painting when arthritis in her fingers made it difficult for her to continue knitting. Later, we will see that other artists made similar adaptations. And this brings us to Pruyser's article on the creativity of older persons.

---

12. Ibid., 318–21. His later book, *The Play of the Imagination,* is based on this three-part model. Strongly influenced by D. W. Winnicott's "Transitional Objects and Transitional Phenomena," it includes chapters on illusion processing in the visual arts, literature, the sciences, religion, and music.

13. Pruyser, "An Essay on Creativity," 343.

The Connection between Creativity and Mourning

Pruyser begins "Creativity in Aging Persons" with the following observation:

> Advanced age is often described as the life stage characterized by loss or decline of various bodily and mental functions, by reduction of energy, and, frequently, by downward shifts in social and financial status. Getting old not only entails these particular losses, but also often prompts disappointments, produces a mood of malcontent or leads to unwanted separation from loved ones; in a word, it can do damage to one's acquired pattern of meanings and values.[14]

Some of these losses are due to the deaths of persons who are meaningful to us, while others involve our own mental and physical functioning:

> In old age, when loved ones, peers, and friends have a high incidence of dying, we are frequently faced with heavy mourning tasks for the lost ones while we are already mourning the loss of the functions of our own mind and body and the reduction of our ego's competence. We are also likely to feel apprehensive about the blows to the integrity of our self and our sense of meaning.[15]

Given these losses and the mourning that accompanies them, we may wonder how there can be any creativity in this stage of life. And yet, Pruyser points to psychoanalytic studies of gifted persons in the arts, music, literature and other cultural domains that indicate a close psychodynamic connection between mourning and creativity. He specifically cites Freud's study of Leonardo da Vinci, "the first of a whole genre of psychoanalytic literature that centers on the spur that creativity receives in the lives of noted artists and musicians by the tragic loss in their childhood of a parent, sibling, or beloved caretaker, or by some other painful memory."[16] This literature reflects the classical psychoanalytic view that creativity and the development of a talent have the function of memorial-

---

14. Ibid., 425.

15. Ibid., 426. Here, he implicitly invokes Erikson's psychosocial crisis of integrity vs. despair.

16. Ibid., 426. In Freud, *Leonardo da Vinci and a Memory of His Childhood*, Freud focuses on Leonardo's separation from his birth mother, with whom he had lived alone, when he was about three years old, when he became a member of his father's household. Freud also notes that Leonardo was deprived of a father these three years. See also Capps, *At Home in the World*, chap. 1.

izing a lost person or relation and then making a symbolic restitution for that loss in the form of a creative work.

Pruyser notes that "most psychoanalytic views on creativity and mourning arose from retroactive studies of very gifted persons widely considered to have been creative in light of the famous works they produced."[17] On the other hand, there are creative people without conspicuous talent and highly talented persons who are not creative, and this means that "creativity may have unassuming manifestations, yielding no landmark works while yet elevating the quality of mind or life of such creative 'ordinary people' and possibly the lives of some other beneficiaries as well."[18] Thus, the intention of his article is to focus on the creativity of "ordinary" aging people, not those with "conspicuous talent."

Old-Age Problems, Tasks, and Issues and Their Bearing on Creativity

Having identified the focus of his study of creativity in aging persons, Pruyser cites W. B. Yeats's poem titled "The Four Ages of Man":[19]

> He with body waged a fight,
> But body won; it walks upright.
>
> Then he struggled with the heart;
> Innocence and peace depart.
>
> Then he struggled with the mind;
> His proud heart he left behind.
>
> Now his wars on God begin;
> At stroke of midnight God shall win.

Noting that the poem represents old age as having "problems and tasks and issues all its own, different from earlier stages," Pruyser suggests that the question then becomes, "What are some of these and what might be their bearing on creativity?"[20] He identifies five features of older adulthood that are particularly relevant to creativity.

17. Pruyser, "An Essay on Creativity," 427.

18. Ibid., 427.

19. Yeats, *Selected Poetry*, 179.

20. Pruyser, "Creativity in Aging Persons," 428.

First, the role and the quality of *aspiration* change in old age. On the whole, there is a reduction in the intensity of striving and straining. In effect, older persons' aspirations are usually not as far ahead of their actual achievements as they were in their youth. Their ambitions "may have been pared down by long exposure to reality and the successive experiences of limitations."[21] At the same time, their true accomplishments may also have raised their competence to a higher level, and they may "feel less urge to accomplish new things or to make their marks anew." On the other hand, since they are much closer to the idea and the time of their own demise, "they may feel the urge to make up for lost opportunities, to set straight past transgressions, or to finally implement some long-cherished but never-realized ideal or wish, possibly with the acute feeling that they are running out of time."[22]

How does this change in aspirations affect their creativity? For some older persons, the quality of mourning over actual or anticipated losses may move them toward a new creativity that reaffirms a past creative work or tendencies. For others, it may come as a complete surprise to themselves and their loved ones. Or the quality of their creative work may change, reflecting the fact that their lives have been touched by loss. Also, their creativity may be more attitudinal than product oriented. For example, it may consist of the enjoyment of writers' and artists' creative works, or it may entail teaching, doing charitable work, or making a wise and socially beneficial will. Or it may simply manifest itself in being an example to others in bearing one's affliction or meeting one's end. On the other hand, it may involve making gifts to others of handiworks that, though not stunning, may yet display considerable skill, a noteworthy aesthetic value, or a cleverly conceived utility, in addition to the valuable self-expression and appreciated contribution to the pleasure and welfare of others.[23]

Second, older persons are, in a special sense, *survivors*: "They have survived hardships, losses, deprivations, calamities, disappointments, setbacks, failures, disillusionments, risky surgeries, and many other unpleasant or life-endangering experiences."[24] The very fact that they are still around is evidence that they are resilient and resourceful, and that they may thus be prepared for the hardships and losses yet to come, includ-

21. Ibid.
22. Ibid.
23. Ibid.
24. Ibid., 429.

ing the final loss of their lives. If they have not been "unduly pampered by Lady Luck and have not been spared exposure to common human unhappiness, they will by now have developed for themselves some sense of what works and does not work, of what they can realistically hope for and what are pipe dreams, of what are essentials and what are trivia."[25] Knowing the difference between what counts in life and what is a mere distraction, some may approach their last years with a special sense of vocation to think and act for the betterment of human society in a variety of different ways, while others may feel called to engage in constructive sociopolitical action, to work for charity, to devote themselves to promoting justice, to oppose tyrannies in any form, or to stand up publicly for unpopular causes. Here, their creativity may be more attitudinal than product oriented. They are to be lauded for courage in taking risks, and their stance and existential involvement are to be valued for their exemplary quality.

Third, older persons show a comparatively *greater interiority* than commonly occurs among younger persons or than occurred in their own younger years. Although some older persons manifest a schizoid withdrawal from the outside world, many develop a special interiority or spiritual self-sufficiency that makes them less dependent than younger people on external stimulation. Such interiority can lead to creative dreaming, meditative musing, deep reflection, or contented solitariness. Although such interiority may manifest itself in splendid works of art, the forms that it takes are predominantly attitudinal, and if this leads "to an attitude of tolerance for diversity, eccentricity, deviancy, or oddity of other people, a whole culture stands to gain from such an example."[26]

Fourth, older persons tend to experience an eventual *waning of oedipal tensions and conflicts*:

25. Ibid.

26. Ibid., 430. In their chapter on "The Voices of Our Informants," in Erikson et al., *Vital Involvement in Old Age*, Erik H. Erikson, Joan M. Erikson, and Helen Q. Kivnick note that the older persons they studied do not, for the most part, center their attention on the large issues of the day: "Instead, they focus on smaller issues, voicing clear ideas about how individual human beings should live—as long as we have the privilege of living at all: 'You have to be tolerant and respect other people's judgments.' 'Respect and kindness are essential.'" The authors suggest that these and other prescriptions voiced by their informants "closely resemble the prescriptions these elders might have received from their own parents or grandparents. They are the principles according to which these people have tried to live their lives, and according to which they now take stock of their pasts, in an effort to move into the future with mature wisdom" (Erikson, et al., *Vital Involvement in Old Age*, 68–69).

> Although the oedipal situation and the relations to which it pertains are likely to remain pertinent throughout the life span, their conflictual intensity waxes and wanes. There comes a time after the parenting tasks have been fulfilled in which parents can accept being equaled, if not bested, by their offspring. There may no longer be any reasons for feelings of rivalry, particularly when ambition is declining anyway and in turn the adult children are now more preoccupied with oedipal relations "downward" with their own children than "upward" to their parents. Having thus moved beyond the oedipal child and parent roles, aging parents can engage in peer relations or friendships with their own progeny.[27]

Pruyser suggests that overcoming enmeshment in oedipal relations can be viewed as a creative advance in its own right. Moreover, "If diminished rivalry in persons with a good record of previous creative activity now leads to a lessening of their creative productivity, such work reduction should not be held against them," for older persons "have a right to seek a quieter life, greater privacy, a smaller range of operations, and some exemption from prevailing hustle and bustle than they were used to, or what the culture accepts as normative."[28] This is especially important in a culture whose adulation of eternal youth already imposes guilt and shame feelings on persons seeking quietude, a culture in which older persons are confronted with a moralistic demand to be "active" and "engaged."

Fifth, old age implies having had *more and more varied experiences* than in earlier life stages, and this means that we may expect that "sensitive and reflective older people will have developed an eye for the ambiguity or tragedy inherent in life's important themes."[29] Thus, "love and hate, life and death, fortune and misfortune, pleasure and pain, freedom and bondage—each of these pairs of terms no longer has one clear and simple meaning." Therefore,

> barring profound characterological rigidity, there may be a softening of earlier dogmatism, perhaps coupled with a live-and-let-live attitude and a forgiving approach to other people's and one's own foibles. Reaching that orientation is no mean maturational gain, and when it leads further to an appreciation of reality as change rather than as a fixed structure, one gets a glimpse, as

27. Pruyser, "Creativity in Aging Persons," 430.

28. Ibid.

29. Ibid.

it were, of Creativity as a cosmic process. Such a glimpse may become a vision that greatly stimulates the imagination.[30]

Pruyser illustrates this appreciation of reality as change rather than as a fixed structure by citing the French psychoanalyst Jacques Lacan's emphasis on the formative role for selfhood in the toddler's discovery of his or her own image in mirrors. Pruyser asks whether there may be a second or final mirror stage in older adulthood, and, if so, what might its impact be? He notes that most people "look at their mirror image all through life and thereby gain various impressions about their vigor, beauty, health, attractiveness, distinction—in a word, about their 'looks'—which affect their self-esteem and satisfy or frustrate their narcissistic needs."[31] Yet, for older persons their mirror image may confirm "that they now look truly *old*, usually from uncomplimentary self-presentations in the glass."[32] Thus, it takes healthy self-respect to accept with equanimity the bodily signs of looking old and feeling old, "but it takes a creative stance of consciousness to discover a unique beauty, dignity, loveliness, or allurement in these same signs—in oneself and in others," and when this occurs, "more is achieved than a bolstered self-esteem." In fact, it is not too much to claim "that a more profound sense of selfhood is gained."[33]

Memory Reorganization and the Creation/Destruction Dialectic

Having set forth the five features of older adulthood that have particular bearing on creativity, Pruyser suggests that many of the points he has made thus far are part of a complex late-life process that may be described as *reorganizing one's memories* or, perhaps more accurately, of *memories reorganizing themselves*, for such reorganization of memory usually occurs involuntarily, as in the faulty recall of names, in word-finding troubles, and in other mnemonic dysfunctions. On the other

30. Ibid. In *The Play of the Imagination*, 207, Pruyser quotes George Santayana's declaration in *The Sense of Beauty*, 117, that "unless human nature suffers an inconceivable change, the chief intellectual and aesthetic value of our ideas will always come from the creative action of the imagination."

31. Pruyser, "Creativity in Aging Persons," 431.

32. Ibid. Pruyser has reference here to Lacan's "The Mirror Stage as Formative of the Function of the I as Revealed in Psychoanalytic Experience."

33. Pruyser, "Creativity in Aging Persons," 431.

hand, when images of recent events become foggy while a contrastingly good recall of more remote events is maintained, "one may see in such apparent breakdown also an organismic wisdom at work that discards trivia so as to guard valuables."[34]

Thus, to all aging persons comes the existential question of what they are to dwell on with the aid of memory, of what is to be kept vivid and what is to be discarded voluntarily and involuntarily. But whatever the causes and mechanisms involved may be, "it would appear to be a creative attitude in old age to register memory changes with interest (in addition to irritation) and to learn from them one's own existential agenda for this stage of life."[35] In fact,

> if Descartes was right in saying that the mind is always busy thinking, and if Freud was correct in holding that nothing experienced is ever radically forgotten, repression is by no means only a pathological aberration; it is also a major health maintenance device that makes growth possible by periodic housecleaning of the inner life and by age-appropriate rearrangements of the mind's furniture.[36]

In other words, forgetting, in some cases at least, has a survival function.

Pruyser also notes that *every act of creation is also in some sense an act of destruction.* The new opposes the old, overcomes tradition, and makes previous novelties obsolete. If creative artists, scientists, and inventors have always had to battle the authority of custom or ignore the establishment in their particular field, so aging persons "may find themselves destroying, in their creative moves, old and useless ideas they once espoused but which now appear as impediments to their future maturing."[37] Although some older persons may become more rigid as they increase in years, aging makes others freer, enabling them to espouse progressive ideas and causes. Thus, aging persons may develop a liberationist ethic as they wrestle themselves free from external patterns of thought control to which they once more or less willingly submitted: "One begins to see the oppressiveness or stifling aspects of professional codes, the phoniness of always trying to 'make a good impression,' or the falsehood of keeping up appearances." Thus, many aging persons look at

34. Ibid.
35. Ibid., 431–32.
36. Ibid., 432.
37. Ibid.

retirement not merely as an opportunity "to do what they have always wanted to do, but more profoundly as a chance to become themselves."[38]

If retirement affords the opportunity to develop a liberationist ethic, Pruyser suggests that increased longevity may also result in the emergence of a situationist ethic. Due to the impressive capacity of the medical profession to prolong the life of the body and to repair malfunctioning organs, many older persons are being forced "to take a second look at what they have thus far regarded as moral or philosophical absolutes."[39] In this regard, the high frequency of suicide in old age is not merely the result of depression in the psychiatric sense but of perfectly normal persons exercising the right to die in dignity and in accord with their psychic timetables. Thus,

> advanced age, especially if beset by illness and handicap, is a time that confronts the person with *the limits of widely held absolutes*; it paints a picture of ambiguity that demands such creative ventures as situation ethics or an "ethics of ambiguity."[40]

It is noteworthy that Pruyser views these new ethical developments as expressions of creativity, a creativity that seems especially to reflect changes in the role and quality of *aspiration* in old age.

Mortality and the Consolations of Humor

Pruyser concludes his article with a brief consideration of *humor*. He suggests that "next to destruction of former impediments to growth and liberation from former fetters and dysfunctional absolutes, the achievement of *humor* is probably one of the greatest forms of creativity within the reach of ordinary people."[41] He notes that humor here "does not mean cracking jokes and engaging in roaring laughter—certainly not at other

38. Ibid. We may note that Pruyser's earlier comments on the *mirror stage* imply the futility of the very attempt to "keep up appearances."

39. Ibid.

40. Ibid., 433. In *Men and Depression*, 41, Sam V. Cochran and Fredric E. Rabinowitz provide a table that indicates the estimated suicide rates per one hundred thousand by age and gender (1992–1997). Suicide rates are considerably higher among men than women at all ages, and women's suicide rates remain quite stable throughout the life span. In the case of men, the highest suicide rates are in older adulthood: age 70–74: 35.5; age 75–79: 46.0; age 80–84: 62.0; age 85+: 75.0. The rates for men between ages 20 and 65 range from 24.3 to 28.5.

41. Pruyser, "Creativity among Aging Persons," 433.

people's expense," but "the capacity to smile benignly at oneself, to accept one's inevitable foibles, and to accept realistically one's limitations in influencing the world without feeling lamed by such awareness."[42]

Among these limitations, one's mortality looms especially large, and "the sure coming of one's own demise is both a fact and a symbol of one's personal life."[43] But the attitude of humor reflects the creativity of self-acceptance in the face of one's mortality. Noting that one popular view of mortality, a view reflected in the concluding line of Yeats's poem, is that of a battle in which victors and victims are made, Pruyser points out that

> Greek mythology approached mortality as a quiescent draft of water from the river Lethe which induces obliviousness of one's past, of one's identity, of one's individuality. Somehow, humor and water are related: Etymologically, humor means liquid, and it is in liquids that substances can be resolved. To prefer the Greek water symbolism to the prevailing battle symbolism of mortality may be humor's greatest gift and consolation.[44]

Thus, Pruyser concludes with an appeal to the creative attitude of humor and, more specifically, to a preference for water symbolism over battle symbolism in relation to mortality, because it invites us to think of humor as a source of consolation in the face of our own impending death.

If humor is a source of consolation in the face of death, how does it accomplish this? Pruyser, who was very familiar with Freud's writings, may well have had Freud's article "Humor" in mind when he proposed that humor is a source of consolation in the face of death, for Freud makes a similar point in this article.[45] In any case, this article is relevant to Pruyser's suggestion that humor can be an important resource for older adults. Following is a brief summary of the points Freud makes in the article on humor.

Freud begins the article with a reference to his much earlier book on humor, to which I referred in the introduction, originally published in 1905.[46] He notes that his objective in the book was to discover the source of the pleasure derived from humor, and says that he thinks he was able to show that the pleasure proceeds from "a saving in expenditure" of

42. Ibid.
43. Ibid.
44. Ibid.
45. Freud, "Humor."
46. Ibid., 263; see Freud, *Jokes and Their Relation to the Unconscious.*

emotion.[47] In a summary statement in the closing paragraph of the book, Freud concluded that the pleasure in jokes arises from saving the expenditure of inhibitions, the pleasure in the comic from saving the expenditure of ideation or thinking, and the pleasure in humor from saving in the expenditure of feeling. Generally speaking, Freud means by *humor* here the ways we make light of life situations that are inherently or potentially painful. If we think of humor more broadly, including jokes, comedy, and amusing observations, we may say that humor saves in the expenditure of *painful emotions, costly inhibitions,* and *difficult thinking.*[48]

In his article "Reflections upon War and Death," published in 1915 during World War I, Freud made the observation that civilized societies require their citizens to live beyond their psychological means, and suggests that this is why neuroses are so common.[49] In other words, we are living on credit, using psychological resources that we do not yet possess. This observation puts in perspective his view that humor saves in the expenditure of painful emotions, costly inhibitions, and difficult thinking, as it means that humor can be a very significant method for retaining possession of our limited yet invaluable psychological resources. Psychologically speaking, humor is money in the bank.

In his article on humor, Freud suggests several ways that the saving in the expenditure of painful emotions may occur. The savings may occur when one adopts a humorous attitude toward oneself, when one witnesses another person's humorous attitude toward himself, or when one person makes a humorous comment about another person. To illustrate how the first two savings in expenditure of emotions work, Freud relates the story

47. Freud, "Humor," 263.

48. *Costly inhibitions* have mainly to do with things we might have said or done but did not do so for fear of social disapproval or punishment. It is often noted that children are much less inhibited than adults because they are more likely to say what is on their minds, at least until they discover that there can be severe sanctions against doing so. Jokes allow one to say things that one would otherwise be forbidden to say or punished for saying. After all, one can claim, I was only joking. *Difficult thinking* has primarily to do with the complexities associated with various professions and occupations that in our own day center on information technologies. There is a whole genre of stupidity jokes going back to the early Egyptians and the Greeks, in which invidious comparisons are made between city and rural inhabitants, or between citizens in geographically adjoining countries. Often these jokes play on prevailing social stereotypes by presenting the presumed stupid person in a positive light, or the presumed intelligent person in a negative light. I have written about this issue in Capps, *A Time to Laugh,* 115–28, 132–34; and Capps, *Laughter Ever After,* chapter 3.

49. Freud, "Reflections upon War and Death," 117.

of the criminal being led to the gallows on a Monday morning who comments, "Well, this is a good beginning to the week." Here, the criminal
saves in the expenditure of his painful emotions by making a humorous
quip, and the quip may also enable one or more of the observers of the
execution to do the same. This is because the observers anticipate that
the victim will show signs of some painful emotions—whether anger,
complaint, manifest pain, fear, horror, or even despair, and are prepared
to follow the victim's lead and call up the same emotions. But when the
victim makes a joke, the observers experience a saving of expenditure in
feeling and may even derive pleasure from it.

Because humor saves in the expenditure of painful emotions, Freud
suggests that it has a *liberating* effect:

> It refuses to be hurt by the arrows of reality or to be compelled
> to suffer. It insists that it is impervious to wounds dealt by the
> outside world, in fact, that these are merely occasions for afford-
> ing it pleasure. This last trait is a fundamental characteristic of
> humor.[50]

Freud notes that the criminal *could* have said as he was being led to the
gallows: "It doesn't worry me. What does it matter, after all, if a fellow
like me is hanged? The world won't come to an end." If he had done so,
we would have to admit that this speech displays the same ability to rise
above the situation and, furthermore, that what he says is wise and true.
But it is not humorous. In fact, it reveals what is distinctive about humor:
that it is not resigned, but rebellious in its refusal to submit to the supe-
rior power of reality itself.

In its refusal to undergo suffering, humor joins other means of re-
fusing to suffer, but unlike delusional thinking it does not leave the world
of mental sanity, and unlike intoxication, it does not attempt to dull the
senses. The criminal being led to the gallows has a moment of pleasure by
saving himself the expenditure of painful emotions. He says, in effect, that
reality—in this case, the reality of death itself—is not powerful enough to
deny him this final moment of pleasure. Freud suggests that what has tak-
en place here is "the ego's victorious assertion of its own invulnerability."[51]
He adds that under ordinary circumstances the superego would tell the
ego that it has no basis for making such a victorious assertion. But here,
the superego abandons its ordinary position as the "stern master" and

50. Freud, "Humor," 265.
51. Ibid.

shows a side of itself that seems rather out of character. It embraces the very humor that we would have thought it would soundly condemn and it "winks at affording the ego a little gratification."[52]

Freud also suggests that "in bringing about the humorous attitude, the superego is in fact repudiating reality and serving an illusion."[53] After all, the criminal's comment about this being a nice way to begin the week has no practical effect on the fact that he is being led to the gallows. Conceivably, the men who are leading him there would find his comment amusing, but they will still continue to lead him to the gallows. Or, if they are humorless and consider his comment rather flippant (after all, they are engaged in the punishment of a man for a crime that warrants his execution), they might even quicken their steps.

But despite the fact that the humor does not change anything as far as reality itself is concerned, "we feel it to have a peculiarly liberating and elevating effect." Besides, the jest made in humor is not the essential thing:

> The principal thing is the intention which humor fulfils, whether it concerns the subject's self or other people. Its meaning is: "Look here! This is all this seemingly dangerous world amounts to. Child's play—the very thing to jest about!"[54]

Freud acknowledges, therefore, that "if it is really the superego which, in humor, speaks such kindly words of comfort to the intimidated ego, this teaches us that we have still very much to learn about the nature of that energy."[55] But one thing is clear: "If the superego does try to comfort the ego by humor and to protect it from suffering, this does not conflict with its derivation from the parental function."[56] It is as if a parent who ordinarily insists that the child adhere to the parent's rules and regulations were to deliberately look the other way when the child violates a rule or

---

52. Ibid., 268. In Freud's terminology, the *ego* is the part of Freud's tripartite division of the mind (*id, ego* and *superego*) that represents the conscious self, the part which reacts to the stimuli of the external world. It is also in constant conflict with the demands of the *id*, which is that part of the mind which is primitive, instinctual, and constitutes the unconscious. The *superego* is the part of the mind which incorporates parental standards and social rules, thus creating conscience and obedience to externally applied laws and regulations. See Rennison, *Freud and Psychoanalysis*, 85, 87, and 89.

53. Ibid., 268.

54. Ibid.

55. Ibid.

56. Ibid., 269.

regulation, and does so because the parent can see that the child is feeling vulnerable or overwhelmed by the external world or some especially threatening aspect of it. In effect, what has occurred here is that humor has created a bond between the superego and the ego, and this is no small accomplishment.

Freud concludes his article on humor with the observation that not everyone is capable of the humorous attitude: "It is a rare and precious gift, and there are many people who have not even the capacity for deriving pleasure from humor when it is presented to them by others."[57] Pruyser's suggestion that humor is a form of creativity is especially relevant here, for although Freud is certainly right in his view that not everyone is capable of the humorous attitude, the very idea that it is a form of creativity accessible to ordinary individuals suggests that one is never too old to develop the humorous attitude. In fact, in light of Pruyser's suggestion that creativity is often found among older persons, it may be more accurate to say that many people are simply too young—or not nearly young enough—to develop the humorous attitude that is far more prevalent— and necessarily so—among aging persons.

Adaptability as a Quality of Creativity

As Pruyser makes clear, his essay on the creativity of older persons is not about individuals we associate with creativity, such as painters and musicians. Rather, he is concerned to identify the creative ways older adults deal with the challenges they confront in older adulthood. In this sense, creativity is eminently practical. On the other hand, I believe that we can learn a great deal about the role that adaptation—both attitudinal and productive—plays in the creative life of the older adult by considering noteworthy artists and the ways they sustained their creativity despite the physical effects of the aging process.

In *The World through Blunted Sight*, Patrick Trevor-Roper, a British eye surgeon, examines the work of well-known artists from the perspective of the physiology of vision.[58] He discusses a range of visual defects, and one of the issues he explores is how changes in vision that occur in later life affect the work of noteworthy painters. Thus, in his consideration of the artists who suffer from presbyopia (or long-sightedness) he points

57. Ibid. 268–69.
58. Trevor-Roper, *The World through Blunted Sight.*

to "the natural weakness of focusing that comes with middle-age which causes a difficulty with near-vision."[59] There is a certain fuzziness in the late paintings of most relatively long-lived artists, such as Rembrandt and Titian. In some cases, this is because "artists simply find detailed work too difficult in old age [and] are often forced to work in a broader way, because their hands, nerves and senses become less responsive (Renoir even tried plastering his paintbrush to his arthritic fingers)."[60]

Trevor-Roper's allusion to Renoir's arthritic fingers recalls our observation in the introduction that Mary Robertson Moses turned to painting, which she had enjoyed as a child, when arthritis in her fingers made it difficult for her to continue knitting. As Jane Kallir points out, "arthritis made it difficult for her to wield a needle, and when her sister Celestia commented that it might be less painful to paint, she really took to the suggestion."[61] After her husband's death in 1927 when she was sixty-seven years old, she made pictures for family members and friends but did not consider painting a full-time occupation. She said she "did it for pleasure, to keep busy and pass the time away."[62] In 1938 her work was accidently discovered by Louis J. Caldor, an amateur art collector, in the drugstore in Hoosick Falls, New York, where she lived. He brought her work to the attention of Otto Kallir, who held an exhibition of her work at his art gallery in New York City in 1940. The exhibition was subsequently reassembled for a Thanksgiving festival at Gimbel's Department Store, and Moses was persuaded to come for the event. Newspapers picked up the story of "Grandma Moses" so that at age eighty she became a house-hold name.[63]

Trevor-Roper notes that in cases where artists experience alterations in their hands, nerves, and senses, their difficulties are often exacerbated by visual defects. For example,

> Michelangelo became nearly blind in old age (wrongly attrib-uted to "strain" from his exacting work). Piero della Francesca became blind "through an attack of catarrh" at sixty. [Honoré] Daumier gave up drawing when he was sixty-nine, when he had an unsuccessful cataract extraction. And, because of failing

59. Ibid., 45

60. Ibid.

61. Kallir, *Grandma Moses*, 12.

62. Ibid., 12.

63. I have written about her painting *Little Boy Blue* in Capps, *At Home in the World*, chapter 8.

sight, Leonardo's later drawings became less detailed, and he re-
linquished his fine silver pencil in favor of a red and blue crayon,
which he could see more readily.[64]

Although these and other artists may have been suffering from other
visual problems, the frequent change in their later works "may well be
attributed in part to a presbyopia that must have rendered the lines of
their canvases increasingly ill-defined."[65] The striking contrast between
"the usual delicacy of detail and refinement of feature" in Rembrandt's
earlier paintings and the face in his self-portrait, painted at the age of
sixty-three and some months before he died, is a case in point. Trevor-
Roper does not mean to suggest that these losses are entirely due to "the
receding near-point of the artist's clear-vision," but he believes that these
visual changes "bear something of the blame—or indeed the credit—for
this (generally advantageous) change in style."[66] His suggestion that the
changes in the style of these painters' later works was "generally advantageous" and his attribution of these changes, at least in part, to visual loss
is an illustration of a point made in chapter 4: that losses experienced in
older adulthood may be responsible for unexpected gains.

   In his discussion of macular degeneration, Trevor-Roper notes that
this degenerative change in vision "dulls and distorts, and finally blots
out the details of the object to which the eye is directed, leaving the rest
of the field of vision unblemished."[67] He does not cite specific examples
of painters whose work in later life was affected by macular degeneration,
but Michael F. Marmor and James G. Ravin, both professors of ophthal-
mology, indicate in their book *The Artist's Eyes* that when the American
painter Georgia O'Keefe (1887–1986) was seventy-seven years old, she
had an experience of vision loss while driving her Buick convertible that
led to the diagnosis of macular degeneration. They compare her *Black
Rock with Blue Sky and White Clouds* painted when she was eighty-seven
with similar, earlier works, such as *Red and Pink Rocks and Teeth,* painted
when she was fifty-one years old, and note that the later painting "has
much less subtlety of shading, and the harsh black shadow is devoid of
gradation," and although "the focus of the picture on a single natural

64. Kallir, *Grandma Moses,* 45.
65. Ibid., 45
66. Ibid., 45, 49.
67. Ibid. 135,

shape is as powerful as ever, the delicacy of shading and contrast that were so characteristic of O'Keefe's earlier work is missing."[68]

They also note that around 1976, when she was eighty-nine years old, O'Keefe began to use assistants to help her paint her canvases. She told one assistant that there were "little holes" in her vision, suggesting that the object that was directly in front of her may not have been visible at all or, at the least, difficult to identify. She was stung by the negative publicity she received when it was revealed that she was using assistants, so she quit using them and increasingly turned to pottery when her vision deteriorated further.

Marmor and Ravin tend to emphasize the negative effects of later-life visual defects on the works of painters discussed in *The Artist's Eyes*. This, of course, is perfectly understandable, because vision loss makes it difficult for artists to see the world as they had previously known it. On the other hand, as we have seen, Trevor-Roper suggests that in the cases of Rembrandt and Titian, changes partly due to visual defects associated with the aging process were "generally advantageous," although he does not discuss this observation in any further detail.

However, Thomas Dormandy has made it the focal point of his book *Old Masters: Great Artists in Old Age*.[69] He argues that many painters and sculptors reached new heights in their seventies and eighties, and did so precisely because they were experiencing the effects of the aging process. Unlike Trevor-Roper and Marmor and Ravin, Dormandy does not focus exclusively on visual diseases and defects (many of which afflicted painters in their earlier years, such as astigmatism and color blindness).[70] On the other hand, Dormandy notes that a painter's style and technique are likely to change in older adulthood, and that such changes are most often due to visual impairments in later life. He cites cases of painters for whom there is clinical evidence of late-age visual impairment (Munch, Reyn-

68. Marmor and Ravin, *The Artist's Eyes*, 201–2.

69. Dormandy, *Old Masters*.

70. Marmor and Ravin, *The Artist's Eyes*, note, for example, that because of his distorted figures, El Greco has been thought by physicians and historians to have suffered from an astigmatism. But when the Duke of Alba sent the American painter John Singer Sargent a booklet written by a Madrid ophthalmologist that argued that El Greco was astigmatic, Sargent disagreed on the grounds that "being very astigmatic myself" and thus "very familiar with the phenomena that result from that peculiarity of eye-sight," it seems "very unlikely that an artist should be influenced by them in the matter of form and not at all in the matter of color where they are much more noticeable" (21–22). Thus, although the argument that El Greco was astigmatic is questionable, Sargent, by his own testimony, was.

olds, Degas, Monet, Dumier, Pisarro, Cassatt) and other painters who most likely suffered from visual impairments (Titian, Chardin, Goya, Turner).

The effect of these impairments on their work is not always clear, but Dormandy cites the interesting case of the twentieth century English painter Edward Ardizzone as presented in Trevor-Roper's *The World through Blunted Sight*. Ardizzone had developed cataracts in both eyes, and his paintings reflected these visual impairments. However, he felt that they reflected a view of the world that was warmer, kinder, and less intense. So he lamented the changes that occurred *after* he underwent surgery on one eye and worried about what would happen when he had surgery on the other eye. As he said to Trevor-Roper:

> Through my operated eye I see a much colder, brighter world, in which reds become pink, greens greener, and blue more intense. At first the difference was startling . . . Everything looks bigger and closer; . . . and then the hardness and brightness; in looking, for instance, at a face, one sees too much: The down on the lip, every wrinkle and pimple, and the stubble of a beard. This wealth of detail makes it difficult to sort out the wood from the trees . . . I am rapidly getting used to the new vision and am unconsciously making all sorts of adjustments. All the same, when my second eye is operated on, I am going to miss the smaller, kinder and rather misty world I have loved so well.[71]

Dormandy observes that in his own view, "the effect of the operation remains wholly undetectable when works painted before and after are compared," but this "does not mean that the techniques of old artists do not change as a result of old age; nor even that one cannot sense in the late years the unforgiving weight of passing years."[72] And yet, he notes that in the very last sketches by the French painter Claude Lorain, the "pen strokes as well as the brush strokes become noticeably shaky; but their tremulousness under the blue, grey and green washes give them a delicacy even he had never achieved before."[73]

Dormandy also notes that one witnesses "a similar kind of dissolution in Michelangelo's last drawings," notably his black chalks of the *Crucified Christ* and of the *Madonna*: "Their hesitancy is a pale reflection

---

71. Trevor-Roper, *The World trough Blunted Sight*, 96. Quoted in Dormandy, *Old Masters*, 280.

72. Dormandy, *Old Masters*, 280–81.

73. Ibid., 281.

of his once imperial command of line; but genius battling with and transcending physical frailty is a unique, awesome and uplifting experience."[74] The example of Michelangelo, he suggests, may point to a more generally valid reason why physical handicaps could impair technique but never obliterate creative talent. This is the fact that by the time artists have reached their late sixties, seventies, and eighties, they have mastered three extremely complicated processes. First, they have learned to *see* in the real world the raw material of their future paintings, drawings, or sculpture. Second, they have learned to *transform* what they have seen in their minds into the work of art they are about to create. Third, they have learned to *translate* their mental images into actual paintings, drawings or sculpture. Thus, "defects of vision and other physical disabilities merely added a fourth skill to be acquired," that of learning "to circumvent, overcome or cheat the newly imposed limitations." This, Dormandy adds, was not always easy. In fact, "sometimes it must have been fearfully difficult—but compared to the other three, it was child's play."[75]

Here, Dormandy uses the same expression—"child's play"—that Freud uses to convey the superego's consoling words via humor to the beleaguered ego. But there is a sense in which all four processes are essentially "child's play" for, as Pruyser shows, the creative person manifests three dimensions—*playfulness, curiosity,* and *pleasure seeking*—that have their roots and origins in early childhood.[76] It seems rather apparent that the three complicated processes that Dormandy identifies—of *seeing, transforming,* and *translating*—are manifestations of these three dimensions. Thus, if the fourth process of *adaptation* is "child's play" to the experienced artist, this is undoubtedly because it has always been integral to the development of the other three processes. The older creative person may experience adaptation to be more challenging than in earlier stages of life, but this process is not an unfamiliar one.

It should also be emphasized that the three processes of *seeing, transforming,* and *translating* which artists have mastered well before their late sixties, seventies, and eighties are not unique to artists. In fact, this is precisely where Pruyser's view that we should not make a distinction between the creativity of "ordinary" persons and those of "conspicuous talent" is especially relevant. For whatever may be or have been one's

---

74. Ibid.
75. Ibid.
76. Pruyser, "Creativity in Aging Persons," 341.

occupation in life, there was the same need to *see, transform, translate,* and *adapt.*

I would like to conclude these reflections on artists as illustrative of the role that adaptability plays in the creativity of older adults with a brief comment on the portrait paintings by the American painter Thomas Eakins, who was born in 1844, died in 1916, and lived throughout his life in Philadelphia. His portrait paintings provide an example of an artist *transforming* what he sees in his mind when he views an object in the real world—an example particularly relevant to older adulthood.

In her discussion of Eakins's portrait of Walt Whitman, who lived across the Delaware River in Camden, New Jersey, Elizabeth Johns observes, "Of all the material forces to which human beings were subject, perhaps the most obvious, and painful, was that of age—of 'wear'—and Eakins did not hesitate to show a sitter as frankly old."[77] Whitman "had insisted that no real distinctions existed between him and other men and so Eakins showed him in just that way, an old man, like other old men."[78] In fact, because Eakins wanted to make the point that Whitman "was a creature made of earth, an old creature . . . he exaggerated that age to make his point unmistakable." Johns also notes that Eakins would portray persons who were not already old as older than their actual chronological age. This was one of the ways that he could present his subjects as "vulnerable on every front: to disease, to irrationality, to sorrow."[79] Thus, Eakins asked one of his sitters, Walter C. Bryant, "if he could make him look older 'to do a fine piece of work as a work of art and not a likeness.'" Photographs that were taken of other sitters at the time that he was doing their portraits "suggest that a room full of Eakins' portraits is a room full of prematurely older sitters," and "one of Eakins' portraits was noted by those who saw it frequently as 'getting to look more and more like the sitter every year.'"[80] The fact that many of Eakins's sitters "were enraged when they saw the finished portrait" suggests that they did not consider his *transformation* and *translation* of what he *saw* to be especially flattering. In fact, many of his portraits were in his possession when he died

77. Johns, *Thomas Eakins,* 163.

78. Ibid. Johns is referring here, of course, to Whitman's well-known poem, *Song of Myself,* which focuses on his identification with the many persons from all walks of life that he has encountered in his life. See Whitman, *Selected Poems,* 15–84.

79. Johns, *Thomas Eakins,* 165.

80. Ibid., 163–64.

because the sitter or the family member who had commissioned it had
refused to accept it.

Yet it is significant that, to Eakins, the aging of the sitter was integral
to his desire to produce "a work of art," and not a mere likeness which,
after all, a photograph could easily provide. Moreover, the fact that a
sitter came to look more and more like the portrait as time went on is
testimony to the fact that Eakins was able not only to *see* but to *foresee*.
As Erik Erikson notes in *Toys and Reasons*,

> If childhood play and . . . other spheres of playfulness . . . depend
> on a strong visual element, they are also dominated by an almost
> visionary fascination with the temporal fate of figures meaning-
> fully arranged in a circumscribed "world." *This combines the two
> meanings of vision, namely, the capacity to see what is before us,
> here and now, and the power to foresee what, if one can only be-
> lieve it, might yet prove to be true in the future.*[81]

We might also note that in painting his subjects as older than they are,
Eakins was implicitly expressing the idea that they will live into their
older adulthoods, that he saw in their faces that they were survivors.

Conclusion

Pruyser does not specifically discuss the dimensions of creative persons
identified in his earlier essay on creativity in his article on creativity in
aging persons. But it is evident that he views older persons' creativity as
reflecting qualities of *playfulness, curiosity,* and *pleasure seeking.* These
qualities do not serve the purpose of mere distraction from or evasion
of the difficulties and problems that present themselves in older adulthood. On the contrary, they enable the older person to deal creatively
with these difficulties and problems. In this way, the older person makes
use of qualities that were developed in early childhood. It is important
to note in this connection that these qualities manifest themselves in a
variety of ways and in various combinations. Also, I believe we need to
be cautious about trying to specify their role in relation to any specific
difficulty or problem with exactitude and rigor, for even as the creativity
of older adults is more attitudinal than productive, so the influence of the
qualities of *playfulness, curiosity* and *pleasure seeking*—and I would add

---

81. Erikson, *Toys and Reasons*, 46 (italics added).

adaptability—has mostly to do with attitudinal changes, and whether or not a specific problem or difficulty can be solved or overcome, these attitudinal changes have their own life-promoting effects.

What especially comes through in Pruyser's discussion of creativity in older persons is that the creativity is reflected in a greater tolerance than was typical of the individual in earlier years. This tolerance is reflected in attitudes toward others but is also reflected in attitudes toward oneself. For example, one allows oneself a reduction in the intensity of striving and straining, of keeping up appearances, of struggling to remember, of adhering to moral absolutes, and even of taking one's own demise with utter seriousness. This spirit of tolerance toward self and others would not emerge, much less become a prevailing attitude, were it not for the qualities of playfulness, curiosity, pleasure seeking, and adaptability—qualities for which older adults can thank the child who lives inside of them.

In this regard, I cannot help but think that the increase in *interiority* that Pruyser identifies among older persons is fundamentally a rediscovery of this very child. This is not to dispute his claim that the older person shows a comparatively greater interiority than occurs among the mass of younger persons or than occurred in their own younger years. Rather, it is to make the additional claim that central to this newly developed interiority is the experience of self-discovery, particularly the discovery—or rediscovery—of one's child-self. And what better time to make this rediscovery than in one's older adulthood?[82]

82. In his address "Psychoanalytic Reflections on Einstein's Centenary" presented at the centennial symposium in Jerusalem in honor of Albert Einstein, Erik Erikson focused on what he called "the *victorious child* in Einstein" (151). He points to the ways Einstein "succeeded in saving the child in himself" (155) as he grew older, and suggests that "one can celebrate today all at once a childhood leading to unique creativity, a man's singular understanding of what the link of childhood and maturity can mean, *and* his time's public and almost mystical appreciation of the child in him, no matter how much or how little people understood his work" (156). It is noteworthy that Erikson suggests that Einstein's creativity as an adult was directly related to his success in "saving the child in himself."

PART 3

The Artistry of Aging

6

Relaxed Bodies, Emancipated Minds, and Dominant Calm

· · · · ·

Relax: to make looser or less firm or tense, to rest from

Emancipated: set free from restraint or control; released from supervision

Calm: lack of agitation or disturbance; tranquil

Energy: potential forces, inherent power, capacity for vigorous action

· · · · ·

THIS IS THE FIRST of two chapters on the artistry of aging. These two chapters are based on the idea that if older adults are creative persons, it naturally follows that the aging process itself is a form or expression of artistry. The dictionary defines *artistry* as "artistic quality, ability, or work."[1] I have all three—quality, ability, and work—in mind when I suggest that the aging process is a form or expression of artistry. If, as we saw in the preceding chapter, creativity is attitudinal as well as productive,

1. Agnes et al., eds., *Webster's New World College Dictionary*, 81.

we may think of the artistry in the aging process in much the same way, that although it can be expressed in abilities that manifest themselves in work (e.g., projects of various kinds), it may also be revealed in qualities (e.g., the manner in which an older adult relates to others). In these two chapters, I will be focusing more on the qualitative than the productive expressions of artistry in aging. Moreover, it will be evident to readers, as it is to me, that these two chapters merely scratch the surface of these qualitative expressions of artistry. Also, they especially focus on the individual artist and on the attitudinal factors involved in the formation and ongoing development of one's artistry. How one expresses this artistry in one's relations with others is beyond the scope of the present book.

In this chapter I suggest that the artistry of aging is reflected in how we, in effect, compose ourselves. Drawing on two articles by William James, I will propose that we would do well to compose ourselves in terms of three qualities: physical relaxation, mental emancipation, and emotional calm. In chapter 7, I will focus on the issue of mood and will use the Disney film *Snow White and the Seven Dwarfs* to explore the fact that we are composed of several selves, and that there are likely to be conflicts between two or more of these selves. Thus, chapter 7 is concerned with a fourth quality, that of self-reconciliation.

The articles by William James that I will be focusing on in this chapter were not written for older adults. In fact, the first article was written for young women who were embarking on a teaching career, and the second was an address at a philosophical conference. But I believe that these writings enable us to think about the aging process in a creative way. Also, in light of the fact that one of the qualities of the creativity of older adults is *adaptability,* readers of this chapter will see ways in which these articles are adaptable to the life of the older adult.

William James was born on January 11, 1842, and died of heart failure on August 26, 1910, at the age of sixty-eight.[2] As I am using age

---

2. When Sigmund Freud came to the United States in 1909 with C. G. Jung to deliver lectures at Clark University in Worcester, Massachusetts (he was fifty-three at the time), James came to hear their lectures. In *An Autobiographical Study,* Freud mentions that meeting with William James "made a lasting impression upon me," and goes on to say, "I shall never forget one little scene that occurred as we were on a walk together. He stopped suddenly, handed me a bag he was carrying and asked me to walk on, saying that he would catch me up as soon as he had gotten through an attack of angina pectoris which was just coming on. He died of that disease a year later: and I have always wished that I might be as fearless as he was in the face of approaching death" (99).

seventy as the official year of entry into older adulthood, this would mean that James did not quite make it to older adulthood. On the other hand, he would have been considered an older adult in the era in which he lived.

The articles that I will be using here are "The Gospel of Relaxation," which is based on an address James gave to the 1896 graduating class of the Boston Normal School of Gymnastics, and which was published in *Scribner's Magazine* in 1889; and "The Energies of Man," which was his presidential address delivered at Columbia University on December 28, 1906, to the American Philosophical Association. It was published in *The Philosophical Review* in 1907.[3]

The Subject of Mental Hygiene

As noted above, "The Gospel of Relaxation" was written for the 1896 graduating class of the Boston Normal School of Gymnastics. A normal school was a school for high-school graduates who were planning to become elementary-school teachers. It was usually a two-year program, and the student body would have been composed exclusively of women. Linda Simon points out in her biography of William James that he was a very popular lecturer at women's colleges and normal schools, and that "The Gospel of Relaxation" was one of three lectures he gave at Wellesley, Vassar, Bryn Mawr, and several normal schools. The others were "What Makes a Life Significant" and "On a Certain Blindness in Human Beings." Simon notes:

> The message of these talks was self-trust, tolerance, and, above all, joy in living. Earnest young women, embracing unreflectively the religious and moral ideals of the past, responded to the ills of the world with feelings of sadness and despair. James urged them to look more closely at the reality of other people's lives, to understand that happiness may be enjoyed by poor as well as rich, and to recognize that ideals, changing as the world changes, needed to be tested against experience.[4]

3. James, "The Gospel of Relaxation"; James, "The Energies of Men."

4. Simon, *Genuine Reality*, 267. These three lectures were published in his book *Talks to Teachers and to Students on Some of Life's Ideals* in 1899. They composed the section on talks to students. The talks to teachers, which focused on educational psychology, began with a chapter on "Psychology and the Teaching Art." See James, *Writings, 1878–1899*, 705–885.

James states his topic in his opening sentence: "I wish in the following hour to take certain psychological doctrines and show their practical application to mental hygiene—to the hygiene of our American life more particularly."[5] He suggests that Americans, especially those in academic circles, are turning toward psychology these days with great expectations, but if psychology is to justify these expectations, it must do so "by showing fruits in the pedagogic and therapeutic lines."[6] In other words, it has to show that it has value in the areas of education and mental health.

The Body's Influence on Our Emotional and Mental States

Next, James introduces the Lange-James theory of emotions. He presented this theory in his 1884 article "What Is an Emotion?"[7] The following year Carl Lange, a Danish psychologist and physician, presented the same theory in his book on emotions.[8] According to this theory, emotions are due to "organic stirrings" aroused in us by the stimulus of an exciting object or situation. For example, fear is not the direct effect of the feared object's impression on our minds. Instead, it is an effect of an earlier physiological response excited by the object. In other words, we do not run away because we feel afraid, but we feel afraid because we run away. In practical terms, this means that we can indirectly regulate our emotions by regulating these physiological responses.

Also, because our physiological responses are under the direct control of our will, we have a better capacity to exercise control over our emotions by regulating our physiological responses than by trying

5. James, "The Gospel of Relaxation," 825.

6. Ibid., 825.

7. James, "What Is an Emotion?"

8. In his chapter on William James in *Historical Introduction to Modern Psychology*, Gardner Murphy writes: "In 1885 a strikingly similar view was independently offered by the Danish physiologist Carl Lange, who described the physiology of fear, rage, and the like, and arrived at the conclusion that emotions are based simply and solely upon such physiological changes. For him, the nineteenth-century distinction between mentally aroused and physically aroused emotions was meaningless; in fact, it was difficult to find any emotions which were not 'physically aroused.' Bodily changes, especially those of the vascular system, not only gave rise to, but wholly determined, the nature of each emotional state. The general similarity of this to James's view led to the habit of designating as the 'James-Lange theory' the assertion that emotions are simply the manifestations in consciousness of a tide of sensory impressions from skeletal muscles, viscera, and other organs" (199–200).

to regulate our emotions more directly. For example, if we want to feel kindly toward someone with whom we have quarreled, we should make a conscious effort to smile, make sympathetic inquiries and force ourselves to say congenial things. If, instead, we wrestle with our negative feelings toward this person, this will merely draw our attention to these feelings and no change will occur.

We might have expected James to support this rather revolutionary theory with citations from his own article on emotions, but instead he cites "an admirable and widely successful little book," Hannah Whitall Smith's *The Christian's Secret of a Happy Life*. He suggests that her book teaches this fundamental lesson on almost every page: "Act faithfully, and you really have faith, no matter how cold and even dubious you may feel." For example,

> "It is your purpose God looks at," writes Mrs. Smith, "not your feelings about that purpose; and your purpose, or will, is there-fore the only thing you need to attend to . . . Let your emotions come or let them go, just as God pleases, and make no account of them either way . . . They really have nothing to do with the matter. They are not the indicators of your spiritual state, but are merely the indicators of your temperament or of your present physical condition." [9]

Next, James turns to an unnamed "Viennese neurologist of consid-erable reputation" (a reference to Sigmund Freud) and says that according to this neurologist, "no physician can get into really profitable relations with a nervous patient until he gets some sense of what this person's *Bin-nenleben* [i.e. buried life] is, of the sort of unuttered inner atmosphere in which his consciousness dwells alone with the secrets of its prison-house."[10] Freud's chapter on psychotherapy in the book on hysteria that he coauthored with Josef Breuer suggests that this means unearthing a

9. Ibid., 826. In her chapter "Difficulties Concerning the Will" in *The Christian's Secret of a Happy Life*, Smith advises her readers to remember that "the real thing in your experience is what your will decides, and not the verdict of your emotions." She adds: "I am convinced that, throughout the Bible, the expressions concerning the 'heart' do not mean the emotions—what we now understand by the word *heart*. They mean the will, the personality of the man, the man's own central self. The object of God's dealings with man is that this 'I' may be yielded up to Him and this central life abandoned to his entire control. It is not the feelings of the man God wants, but the man himself" (72).

10. James, "The Gospel of Relaxation," 827.

patient's sexual fantasies.[11] James, however, is more interested here in the nervous patient's old regrets relating to ambitions and aspirations that were inhibited by emotions of shame and timidity; and localized bodily discomforts which produce "a general self-mistrust and sense that things are not as they should be."[12]

Here, James employs the Lange-James theory of emotions by noting that emotions derive from physiological reactions and responses. However, in this case the emotions are the result not of a physiological reaction to an *external* stimulus (such as a threatening animal) but to an *internal* one, namely, some physical discomfort that gives rise to morbid feelings. And if he endorses Freud's proposal that physicians probe the "buried life" of their patients, this does not mean that they should focus on the distant past. Rather, they should concern themselves with the "inner atmosphere" of the patient's present physical discomfort. The patient's emotional state is the central issue, but its improvement lies in the rehabilitation of the patient's physical condition. James reinforces this point by noting "the effects of a well-toned *motor-apparatus,* nervous and muscular, on our general self-consciousness" and "the sense of elasticity and efficiency that results."[13]

James cites the changes that occurred in the lives of Norwegian women as a result of their taking up skiing, a sport previously reserved for men. As a result, a "revolutionary" change in their lives took place:

> Fifteen years ago the Norwegian women were even more than the women of other lands votaries of the old-fashioned ideal of femininity, the "domestic angel," the "gentle and refining influence" sort of thing. Now these sedentary fireside tabby cats of Norway have been trained, they say, by their snowshoes into lithe and audacious creatures for whom no night is too dark or height too giddy, and who are not only saying good-bye to the traditional feminine pallor and delicacy of constitution, but actually taking the lead in every educational and social reform. I cannot but think that the current tennis and tramping and skating habits and bicycle craze which are so rapidly extending among our dear sisters and daughters in this country are going

11. Breuer and Freud, *Studies on Hysteria,* 255–305.

12. James, "The Gospel of Relaxation," 827. See also Carlin and Capps, "Coming to Terms with Our Regrets."

13. James, "The Gospel of Relaxation," 827.

also to lead to a sounder and heartier moral tone, which will send its tonic breath through all our American life.[14]

One imagines that his audience of women dedicated to teaching gymnastics would have applauded at this point.

James goes on to cite a book he had read years earlier, by an American physician—whose author's name and whose title he no longer recalls—who prophesied that as the social environment changes, humans will be called upon to develop more mental power, and there will be correspondingly less need for physical strength. After all, machines will do all of our heavy work. The author celebrated the prospect of humans no longer needing muscular strength. But James vigorously disagrees:

> I am sure that your flesh creeps at this apocalyptic vision. Mine certainly did so; and I cannot believe that our muscular vigor will ever be a superfluity. Even if the day comes when it is not needed to fight the old heavy battles against Nature, it will still always be needed to furnish the background of sanity, serenity, and cheerfulness to life, to give moral elasticity to our disposition, to round off the wiry edge of our faithfulness, and to make us good-natured and easy of approach. Weakness is too apt to be what the doctors call irritable weakness. And that blessed internal peace and confidence . . . that wells up from every part of the body of a muscularly well-trained human being, and soaks the indwelling of him with satisfaction, is quite apart from every consideration of its mechanical utility, an element of spiritual hygiene of supreme significance.[15]

Here James affirms the integrity of physical and spiritual hygiene.

The Bottled-Lightning Ideal

Having contended that the body has enormous influence on a person's emotional state, James turns his attention to the rather bad physiological habits of Americans. He notes that on a visit to the United States many years ago, Dr. Thomas Smith Clouston, Scotland's "most eminent asylum physician," said that "you Americans wear too much expression on your faces, are living like an army with all its reserves engaged in action, that you take too intensely the trivial moments of life, and ought somehow to

14. Ibid., 828.
15. Ibid., 829.

tone yourselves down."[16] Agreeing that "intensity, rapidity [and] vivacity of appearance" are "something of a nationally accepted ideal," James cites a story he had recently read in a weekly newspaper, in which the author summarized the heroine's charms by observing that "to all who looked upon her an impression of 'bottled lightning' was irresistibly conveyed." James exclaims: "Bottled lightning, in truth, is one of our American ideals, even of a young girl's character!"[17]

He acknowledges that "there are plenty of bottled-lightning temperaments in other countries, and plenty of phlegmatic temperaments here," and that one could argue that the problem about which he is "making such a fuss is a very small item in the sum total of a nation's life and not worth solemn treatment at a time when agreeable rather than disagreeable things should be talked about!"[18] After all, he was speaking at a graduation ceremony!

> But it is not always the material size of a thing that measures its importance; often it is its place and function. One of the most philosophical remarks I ever heard made was by an unlettered workman who was doing some repairs on my house years ago. "There is very little difference between one man and another," he said, "when you get to the bottom of it. But what little there is, is very important." And the remark certainly applies to this case. The general over-contraction may seem small when estimated in foot-pounds, but its importance is immense on account of its *effects on the over-contracted person's spiritual life.*[19]

This conclusion, he points out, follows as a necessary consequence of the theory of emotions he had referred to earlier. He explains:

> For by the sensations that so incessantly pour in from the over-tense excited body the over-tense and excited habit of mind is kept up; and the sultry, threatening, exhausting, thunderous inner atmosphere never quite clears away. If you never wholly give yourself up to the chair you sit in but always keep your leg- and body-muscles half contracted for a rise; if you breathe eighteen or nineteen instead of fifteen or sixteen times a minute, and never quite breathe out at that,—what mental mood *can* you be in but one of inner panting and expectancy, and how can the

16. Ibid., 829–30.
17. Ibid., 830.
18. Ibid., 830–31.
19. Ibid., 831 (italics original).

> future and its worries possibly forsake your mind? On the other
> hand, how can they gain admission to your mind if your brow
> be unruffled, your respiration calm and complete, and your
> muscles all relaxed?[20]

Clearly, the body has a powerful effect on the mind, and it makes an
enormous difference in one's mental state whether one's body is over-
tense and excited or whether it is unruffled, calm, and relaxed. For James,
the latter is much to be preferred over the former.

The Imitative Impulse and Its Remedy

Clouston's observation prompts James to ask, "Now what is the cause of
this absence of repose, this bottled lightning quality of us Americans?"
He considers various explanations, including the variability of the climate
and the work we do and the pace at which we do it. But he believes that
the real explanation lies in what psychologists and sociologists call the
"imitative impulse," which, together with the "inventive impulse," forms
the entire warp and woof of human society. The overtension, jerkiness,
breathlessness, intensity, and agony of expression among us is largely the
result of the imitative impulse: "They are *bad habits,* nothing more or less,
bred of custom and example, born of the imitation of bad models and the
cultivation of false personal ideals."[21] How these fashions and expressions
came about is impossible to trace—he compares them with the idioms of
phrase and dialect peculiar to a given locality—but he is quite certain that
climate and work conditions have little if anything to do with it.

James acknowledges that no type can be wholly disadvantageous,
but "Dr. Clouston was certainly right in thinking that eagerness, breathlessness, and anxiety are not signs of strength: they are signs of weakness
and of bad coordination."[22]He compares two very different types of workers in terms of their accomplishments:

> Your dull unhurried worker gets over a great deal of ground,
> because he never goes backward or breaks down. Your intense,
> convulsive worker breaks down and has bad moods so often that

20. Ibid.
21. Ibid., 832.
22. Ibid.

you never know where he may be when you need his help,—he may be having one of his "bad days."[23]

Moreover, the reason that so many Americans collapse and need to be sent abroad to rest their nerves is not that they work so hard. Rather,

> I suspect that neither the nature nor the amount of our work is accountable for the frequency and severity of our breakdowns, but that their cause lies rather in those absurd feelings of hurry and having no time; in that breathlessness and tension, that anxiety of feature and that solicitude for results, that lack of inner harmony and ease, in short, by which with us the work is so apt to be accompanied . . . These perfectly wanton and unnecessary tricks of inner attitude and outer manner in us, caught from the social atmosphere, kept up by tradition, and idealized by many as the admirable way of life, are the last straws that break the American camel's back, the final overflowers of our measure of wear and tear and fatigue.[24]

James goes on to note that even Americans' voices have a tired and plaintive sound, and we suffer the "wretched trick of feeling tired by following the prevalent habits of vocalization and expression."[25] If talking at a high or tired pitch and living excitedly and hurriedly enabled us to *do* more than we are doing and to do it well, this would at least compensate for continuing in our habitual ways. But, in fact, the very opposite is the case:

> It is your relaxed and easy worker, who is in no hurry, and quite thoughtless most of the while of consequences, who is your efficient worker; and tension and anxiety, and present and future, all mixed up together in our mind at once, are the surest drags upon steady progress and hindrances to our success.[26]

If the imitative impulse is largely responsible for why Americans are the way they are, the remedy, in James's view, is clear: "We must change ourselves from a race that admires jerk and snap for their own sakes, and looks down upon low voices and quiet ways as dull, to one that, on the contrary, has calm for its ideal, and for their own sakes loves harmony,

23. Ibid., 832–33.
24. Ibid., 833.
25. Ibid.
26. Ibid.

dignity, and ease."[27] And how are we to realize this fundamental change? James suggests that there is only one way to improve ourselves, and that is by some of us setting an example that the others may pick up and imitate till the new fashion spreads from east to west. Some persons have a natural advantage in this regard because they are simply more striking personally, but no one is *not* in a position to be imitated by someone. So, "if you should individually achieve calmness and harmony in your own person, you may depend upon it that a wave of imitation will spread from you, as surely as the circles spread outward when a stone is dropped into a lake."[28]

Noting that we do not have to be "absolute pioneers" in this regard, James mentions that there is a new society in New York for the improvement of our national vocalization, and that its views are being publicized in the newspapers:

> And, better still than that, because more radical and general, is the gospel of relaxation, as one may call it, preached by Miss Annie Payson Call, of Boston, in her admirable little volume called *Power Through Repose*, a book that ought to be in the hands of every teacher and student in America of either sex. You need only be followers, then, on a path already opened by others. But of one thing be confident: others still will follow you.[29]

In the opening chapter titled "The Body's Guidance" Call contends that we have perverted Nature's laws as far as our own bodies are concerned, and that "even though our eyes have been opened to a full recognition of such perversion," it is impossible simply to "jump back into the place where the laws work normally through us."[30] Rather,

27. Ibid.

28. Ibid., 834.

29. Ibid., 835. Annie Payson Call was born in 1853 and died in 1940. She was thirty-eight years old when *Power through Repose* was published (1891). It consists of chapters titled "The Body's Guidance," "Perversions of the Body's Guidance," "Rest in Sleep," "Other Forms of Rest," "The Use of the Brain," "The Brain in Its Direction of the Body," "Nervous Strain in Pain and Sickness," "Nervous Strain in the Emotions," "Nature's Teaching," "The Child as an Ideal," "Training for Rest," "Training for Motion," "Mind Training," "The Artistic Side," and "Tests." In her concluding chapter on tests, she cites the case of gymnasts who greatly overtax their muscles on the grounds that their training enables them to accomplish physical feats that others could not possibly perform.

30. Call, *Power through Repose*, 8.

We must climb back to an orderly life, step by step, and the compensation is large in the constantly growing realization of the greatness of the laws we have been disobeying. The appreciation of a natural law, as it works through us, is one of the keenest pleasures that can come to man in this life.[31]

Like James, Call discusses the power of imitation, but she does not recommend that we necessarily imitate other persons. Instead, she advises us to follow Nature's ways, to imitate "the work of quiet and economy, the lack of strain and false purpose, in fine old Nature herself."[32] Thus, while James makes considerable use of nature for metaphorical purposes in his address, noting, for example, that Freud advises physicians to focus on the "inner atmosphere" of their patients' physical discomforts, Call goes one step further and proposes that we turn to Nature as an exemplar of the gospel of relaxation. It is noteworthy in this regard that she views Nature as an older adult ("fine old Nature"). This is itself an excellent characterization of nature, for among the models available to us to experience the aging process, we can hardly improve on "fine old Nature" herself. As Call points out, Nature teaches us, by her own example, that there are times when we may say to ourselves, "I can do this, now that I know how to relax." At the same time, Nature teaches us, again by her own example, that there are times when "the thing is out of reason, and we should say, 'Because I know how to relax, I see that I must not do this.'"[33] As an imitative model, Nature is unparalleled, and despite what we humans have done to her, her longevity speaks for itself.

The Need to Forget Oneself

Having invited his listeners to aspire to be good imitative models, James offers this cautionary note: "If one's example of easy and calm ways is to be effectively contagious, one feels by instinct that the less voluntarily one aims at getting imitated and the more unconscious one keeps in the matter, the more likely one is to succeed."[34] Thus, *"Become the imitable*

---

31. Ibid.
32. Ibid., 165.
33. Ibid., 161.
34. James, "The Gospel of Relaxation," 835.

thing, and you may then discharge your minds of all responsibility for the imitation [and] the laws of social nature will take care of that result."[35]

He points out that "the psychological principle on which this precept is based is a law of very deep and widespread importance in the conduct of our lives, and at the same time a law which we Americans most grievously neglect."[36] This law states that *"strong feeling about one's self tends to arrest the free association of one's objective ideas and motor processes."*[37] The extreme example of this inhibition is found in melancholia, for the melancholic patient "is filled through and through with intensely painful emotions about himself," his mind being "fixed as if in a cramp on these feelings of his own situation, and in all the books on insanity you may read that the usual varied flow of his thoughts has ceased."[38] But an example closer to home is our own experience of how "a great or sudden pleasure may paralyze the flow of thought:

> Ask young people returning from a party or a spectacle, and all excited about it, what it was. "Oh, it was *fine*! It was *fine*! It was *fine*!" is all the information you are likely to receive until the excitement has calmed down. Probably every one of my hearers has been made half-idiotic by some great success or piece of good fortune. *Good*! GOOD! GOOD!! is all we can at such times say to ourselves until we smile at our own foolishness.[39]

Thus, if we want our ideas and volitions to be abundant, varied, and effective, we need to "form the habit of freeing them from the inhibitive influence of reflection upon them, of egoistic preoccupation about their results."[40] This too is a habit that one can learn:

> Prudence and duty and self-regard, emotions of ambition and emotions of anxiety, have, of course, a needful part to play in our lives. But confine them as far as possible to the occasions when you are making your general resolution and deciding on your plans of campaign, and keep them out of the details. When once a decision is reached and execution is the order of the day, dismiss absolutely all responsibility and care about the outcome. *Unclamp*, in a word, your intellectual and practical machinery,

35. Ibid (italics original).
36. Ibid.
37. Ibid (italics original).
38. Ibid.
39. Ibid., 836.
40. Ibid.

and let it run free, and the service it will do you will be twice as good.[41]

To illustrate this *unclamping* of one's intellectual and practical machinery, James returns to Americans' verbal expression, and, more specifically, to the frequent complaint that social life in New England is either less rich and expressive or more fatiguing than it is in some other parts of the world. He suggests that this is largely due to "the over-active conscience of the people, afraid of either saying something too trivial and obvious, or something insincere, or something unworthy of one's interlocutor, or something in some way or another not adequate to the occasion."[42] He asks:

> How can conversation possibly steer itself through such a sea of responsibilities and inhibitions as this? On the other hand, conversation does flourish and society is refreshing, and neither dull on the one hand nor exhausting from its effort on the other, wherever people forget their scruples and take the brakes off their hearts, and let their tongues wag as automatically and ir-responsibly as they will.[43]

Aware that he is speaking to the graduating class at an institution that trains women for careers in teaching, he cites the wisdom of a teach-er whose identity he does not disclose:

> They talk much in pedagogic circles today about the duty of the teacher to prepare for every lesson in advance. To some extent this is useful. But we Yankees are assuredly not those to whom such a general doctrine should be preached. We are only too careful as it is. The advice I should give to most teachers would be in the words of one who is herself an admirable teacher. Pre-pare yourself in the *subject so well that it shall be always on tap*: then in the class-room trust your spontaneity and fling away all further care.[44]

His advice to students would be somewhat similar:

> Just as a bicycle chain may be too tight, so may one's careful-ness and conscientiousness be so tense as to hinder the running of one's mind. Take, for example, periods when there are many

41. Ibid.
42. Ibid.
43. Ibid., 836–37.
44. Ibid., 837 (italics original).

successive days of examination impending. One ounce of good nervous tone in an examination is worth many pounds of anxious study for it in advance. If you really want to do your best at an examination, fling away the book the day before, say to yourself, "I won't waste another minute on this miserable thing, and I don't care an iota whether I succeed or not." Say this sincerely, and feel it; and go out and play, or go to bed and sleep, and I am sure the results next day will encourage you to use the method permanently.[45]

James goes on to mention that he has heard this advice given to a student by Annie Payson Call, from whose book on muscular relaxation, *Power through Repose,* he had previously quoted. Then he cites another book of hers titled *As a Matter of Course* in which "the gospel of moral relaxation, of dropping things from the mind, and not 'caring,' is preached with equal success."[46] He notes, however, that she is not alone in preaching this gospel. He mentions the mind-cure sects, doctors, several authors, and a "whole band of schoolteachers and magazine readers" as evidence that "it really looks as if a good start might be made in the direction of changing our American mental habit into something more indifferent and strong."[47]

Religion the Cure for Worry

Finally, however, James cautions against undue optimism in this regard because the gospel of moral relaxation is likely to come up against a continuing inhibitive factor. This is the tendency of Americans to worry. Worry causes the "inhibition of associations and loss of effective power." And this is where religion comes in:

45. Ibid., 837.

46. Ibid., 837. Call, *As a Matter of Course,* originally published in 1894, covers a range of topics (including physical care, amusements, moods, tolerance, sympathy, one's self, children, and illness), but an especially prominent chapter is the one that concerns itself with false, mistaken, or disagreeable "brain-impressions." Call is confident that the brain-impressions that keep the self in bondage can be eliminated. For example, if we have the habit of being unpunctual and emphasize this habit by deploring it, no real change will take place. If, however, we create a vivid mental picture of ourselves being on time for the next appointment, this picture will impress itself on our minds and free us to arrive on time or even early (Call, *As a Matter of Course,* 20–21).

47. James, "The Gospel of Relaxation," 837–38.

Of course, the sovereign cure for worry is religious faith; and this, of course, you also know. The turbulent billows of the fretful surface leave the deep parts of the ocean undisturbed, and to him who has hold on vaster and more permanent realities the hourly vicissitudes of his personal destiny seem relatively insignificant things. The really religious person is accordingly unshakable and full of equanimity. And calmly ready for any duty that the day may bring forth.[48]

James suggests that this equanimity and calm is "charmingly illustrated" by a small book by Brother Lawrence, a Carmelite friar, who was converted in Paris in 1666. He quotes several paragraphs from Brother Lawrence's book.[49] These paragraphs relate Lawrence's decision to leave his post as a footman, due in part to his physical clumsiness, and his decision to enter the monastery. But, having made this decision, he found that his duties in the monastery (buying wine, working in the kitchen, and so forth) were onerous and also challenging due to his physical disability. Through prayer, however, Lawrence came to a sense of equanimity and calm about his situation. He concludes (writing in the third person):

The goodness of God assured him that he would not forsake him utterly and that he would give him strength to bear whatever evil he permitted to happen to him; and, therefore, that he feared nothing, and had no occasion to consult with anybody about his state. That when he attempted to do so, he had always come away more perplexed.[50]

James comments: "The simple-heartedness of the good brother Lawrence, and the relaxation of all unnecessary solicitudes and anxieties in him, is a refreshing spectacle."[51] As Brother Lawrence's testimony reveals, religious faith enables one to be calmly ready for any duty that the day may bring forth.

James closes the address with the observation that "the need of feeling responsible all the livelong day has been preached long enough in our New England. Long enough exclusively, at any rate,—and long enough to the female sex."[52] This being the case, "what our girl students and

48. Ibid., 838.
49. Brother Lawrence, *The Practice of the Presence of God.*
50. James, "The Gospel of Relaxation," 839.
51. Ibid.
52. Ibid.

their woman teachers most need now-a-days is not the exacerbation, but rather the toning down of their moral tensions."[53] But this raises another concern:

> Even now I fear that some of my fair hearers may be making an undying resolve to become strenuously relaxed, cost what it will, for the remainder of her life. It is needless to say that this is not the way to do it. The way to do it, paradoxical as it may seem, is genuinely not to care whether you are doing it or not. Then, possibly, by the grace of God, you may all at once find that you *are* doing it, and having learned what the trick feels like, you may (again by the grace of God) be enabled to go on. That something like this may be the happy experience of all my hearers is, in closing, my most earnest wish.[54]

Thus, he concludes on a graceful note, as graceful, perhaps, as a member of the audience skating circles on the Charles River on a winter day.[55]

The Energies of Men and Women

In "The Gospel of Relaxation," James was concerned with Americans' misuse of their physical energies and the effects of this misuse on their mental functioning (which includes emotions as well as thoughts and ideas). As he put it, "the over-tense excited body" produces an "excited habit of mind."[56] In "The Energies of Men," he focuses on the fact that Americans do not use the mental resources available to them, explores the reasons for this, and presents some ideas for how they may avail themselves of these energies.

James begins by observing that everyone knows "the difference between the days when the tide of this energy is high in him and when it is low."[57] He acknowledges the difficulty of knowing what reality the term

---

53. Ibid.

54. Ibid., 840.

55. The members of James's audience, especially those, the graduates, to whom his message was particularly addressed, were young. My own most vivid experience of witnessing a graceful skater, however, was of watching a woman who was in her seventies. Also, I have suggested in chapter 3 that the seventies are the decade of *the graceful self.*

56. James, "The Gospel of Relaxation," 831.

57. James, "The Energies of Men," 1224.

energy covers in this regard, and notes that functional psychologists have not been of much help in explaining the difference. But,

> everyone knows on any given day that there are energies slumbering in him which the incitements of that day do not call forth, but which he might display if these were greater. Most of us feel as if we lived habitually with a sort of cloud weighing on us, below our highest notch of clearness in discernment, sureness in reasoning, or firmness in deciding. Compared with what we ought to be, we are only half-awake. Our fires are damped, our drafts are checked. We are making use of only a small part of our possible mental and physical resources.[58]

James notes that part of this imperfect vitality that we experience can be explained by scientific psychology: "It is the result of the inhibition exerted by one part of our ideas on other parts."[59] He points out that conscience makes cowards of us all, and social conventions prevent us from telling the truth. Also, our scientific respectability keeps us from exercising the mystical portions of our nature freely. He laments the fact that he is unable to talk freely about certain topics that are of interest to him with some of his dearest friends because they are inhibited intellectually. The topic "made them too uncomfortable, they wouldn't play, I had to be silent."[60] He contrasts such inhibition with the example of Gustav T. Fechner, "an extraordinary exception that proves the rule":

> He could use his mystical faculties while being scientific. He could be both critically keen and devout. Few scientific men can pray, I imagine. Few can carry on any living commerce with "God." Yet many of us are well aware how much freer in many directions and abler our lives would be, were such important forms of energizing not sealed up. There are in everyone potential forms of activity that are actually shunted out from use.[61]

He suggests that a useful analogy is the phenomenon of the second wind we experience when we seem to have reached the end of our physical endurance. Just when our fatigue seems unendurable, we tap into a new

58. Ibid., 1224–25.

59. Ibid., 1225.

60. Ibid., 1221.

61. Ibid., 1225–26. Fechner was a German physicist-philosopher (1801–1887). James devoted a lecture to Fechner's views in his Hibbert Lectures at Oxford University in 1908. They were published in 1909 under the title *A Pluralistic Universe*. See Capps, *At Home in the World,* 152–55.

level of energy that we did not know we possessed. No doubt, there are other new levels—a third or a fourth wind—as well. The same is true of our mental energies:

> Mental energy shows the phenomenon as well as physical, and in exceptional cases we may find, beyond the very extremity of fatigue distress, amounts of ease and power that we never dreamed ourselves to own, sources of strength habitually not taxed at all, because habitually we never push through the obstruction, never pass those early critical points. . . . We live subject to inhibition by degrees of fatigue which we have only from habit to obey.[62]

In his view, it doesn't have to be this way. Even as psychologists have shown that one can be in nutritional equilibrium, neither losing nor gaining weight, on astonishingly different quantities of food,

> So one can be in what I might call "efficiency-equilibrium" (neither gaining nor losing power when once the equilibrium is reached), on astonishingly different quantities of work, no matter in what dimension the work may be measured. It may be physical work, intellectual work, moral work, or spiritual work.[63]

He acknowledges that there are limits in this regard. After all, the trees do not grow into the sky: "But the plain fact remains that men the world over possess amounts of resource, which only very exceptional individuals push to the extremes of use."[64]

The Release of Inhibited Mental Energies

How might one begin to release—to emancipate—these inhibited mental resources? James identifies three liberating factors that unleash unused mental energies: emotional excitations, efforts of will, and suggestive ideas. To illustrate the effect of emotional excitations, he presents a British military officer's firsthand account of his ability to draw on extraordinary stores of energy during the six-week siege of Delhi in 1857. To illustrate efforts of will, he presents a European friend's firsthand account of how he had been beset with an unstable nervous system that caused

62. James, "The Energies of Men," 1226–27.
63. Ibid., 1227.
64. Ibid.

him to live for many years in a circular process of alternating lethargy and overanimation. He would typically experience three weeks of extreme activity followed by a week of prostration in bed. He decided to try Hatha Yoga, "partly out of curiosity, and partly with a sort of desperate hope."[65] Initially, the program seemed to him to be ineffective. In fact, he had an experience of prostration that was worse than anything he had ever experienced before. But in four months' time he was a new person. As he wrote to James,

> My intuition was developed by these practices: there came a sense of certainty, never known before, as to the things needed by the body and the mind, and the body came to obey like a wild horse tamed. Also the mind learned to obey, and the current of thought and feeling was shaped according to my will.[66]

To James, the recipient of his letters, the most remarkable change was in their moral tone: "Compared with certain earlier letters, these read as if written by a different man, patient and reasonable instead of vehement, self-subordinating instead of imperious."[67]

James also notes that his correspondent made an association between his change and "suggestive therapeutics." James agrees but takes this insight further:

> Call his whole performance, if you like, an experiment in self-suggestion. That only makes it more valuable as an illustration of what I wish to impress in as many ways as possible upon your minds, that we habitually live inside our limits of power. Suggestion, especially under hypnosis, is now universally recognized as a means, exceptionally successful in certain persons, of concentrating consciousness, and, in others, of influencing their body's states. It throws into gear energies of imagination, of will, and of mental influence over physiological processes, that usually lie dormant. And that can only be thrown into gear at all in chosen subjects.[68]

Observing that his friend's experiment shows that "ideas set free beliefs, and the beliefs set free our wills," James says he must now "say

---

65. Ibid., 1231.
66. Ibid., 1233.
67. Ibid., 1235.
68. Ibid., 1234.

a word about *ideas* as our third great dynamogenic agent."[69] This brings us back the topic that I raised in the introduction where I noted that it suddenly dawned on me that older adulthood is a time of growth and development. First, picking up on his earlier discussion, James points out the inhibiting effect of ideas, and elaborates on the complexities involved:

> Ideas contradict other ideas and keep us from believing them. An idea that thus negates a first idea may itself in turn be negated by a third idea, and the first idea may thus regain its natural influence over our belief and determine our behavior. Our philosophic and religious development proceeds thus by credulities, negations, and the negating of negations.[70]

But whether an idea arouses or arrests belief, "ideas may fail to be efficacious, just as a wire at one time alive with electricity, may at another time be dead." The cause in any given case may elude us, but, in general, "whether a given idea shall be a live idea, depends more on the person into whose mind it is injected than on the idea itself."[71] James posits that the foregoing discussion of suggestion and hypnosis is relevant here because it prompts us to ask:

> Which are the suggestive ideas for this person, and which for that? Beside the susceptibilities determined by one's education and by one's original peculiarities of character, there are lines along which men simply as men tend to be inflammable by ideas. As certain objects naturally awaken love, anger, or cupidity, so certain ideas naturally awaken the energies of loyalty, courage, endurance, or devotion. When these ideas are effective in an individual's life, their effect is often very great indeed. They may transfigure it, unlocking innumerable powers which, but for the idea, would never have come into play.[72]

James cites examples of energy-releasing abstract ideas ("Holy Church," "Truth," "Science," and the like) and the oath, vow, or pledge as employed, for example, in the temperance movement. Conversions are another example:

> *Conversions*, whether they be political, scientific, philosophic, or religious, form another way in which bound energies are let

69. Ibid., 1236.
70. Ibid.
71. Ibid.
72. Ibid.

loose. They unify, and put a stop to ancient mental interferences. The result is freedom, and often a great enlargement of power. A belief that thus settles upon an individual always acts as a challenge to his will. But, for the particular challenge to operate, he must be the right challeng*ee*. In religious conversions we have so fine an adjustment that the idea may be in the mind of the challengee for years before it exerts effects; and why it should do so then is often so far from obvious that the event is taken for a miracle of grace, and not a natural occurrence. Whatever it is, it may be a highwater mark of energy, in which "noes," once impossible, are easy, and in which a new range of "yeses" gain the right of way.[73]

The moral effects of religious conversions in general and suggestive ideas in particular prompt James, at this point in the lecture, to discuss the new forms of "spiritual philosophy" then "passing over our American world."[74] He notes that the common feature of these optimistic faiths is that they advocate the suppression of what Horace Fletcher (1849–1919) calls "fear thoughts," which he defines as "the self-suggestion of inferiority."[75] As James points out, when "fear-thought" is suppressed a countersuggestion of power is bound to occur, and this power, whether great or small, "comes in various shapes to the individual."[76]

73. Ibid., 1238 (italics original). As I noted in the introduction, James used the phrase "the letting loose of hope" in his book *Pragmatism*, published in 1907, the same year that "The Energies of Men" was published. In his discussion of the differences between a materialist and a spiritualist view of the universe, he suggests that the effect of the idea of the world "with a God in it" and thus "the affirmation of an eternal moral order" is "the letting loose of hope" (*Pragmatism*, 48–49).

74. James, "The Energies of Men," 1238.

75. Ibid. James's source for this reference is Fletcher's *Happiness as Found in Forethought Minus Fear-thought*, 24–25. Here, Fletcher notes that various psychologists have shown that "the consideration of the future that constitutes *forethought* is a mixture of hope, faith and fear, the sum of which is the stimulant to action and progress" (23). He claims, however, that what he himself has shown is that the fear necessary in earlier stages of human history is unnecessary today, and as soon as it becomes unnecessary, it is a deterrent to action and progress. What he has demonstrated beyond the possibility of doubt is that "*the fear element can be eliminated* out of forethought *as soon as it becomes evident that it is unnecessary, separable and eliminable, and that energy and desire for progress and growth are beautifully stimulated as the result of its elimination*"(24, italics original). See also Carlin and Capps, *100 Years of Happiness*, chapter 1.

76. James, "The Energies of Men," 1238.

To illustrate this countersuggestion of power, James cites the case of a friend, the "most genuinely saintly person I have ever known," who has breast cancer. However, she has rejected the advice of her doctors. (He does not indicate what they advised.) James says that it is not for him to judge whether this is wise or not, but the point he wants to make is that she is "an example of what ideas can do," providing that they are the right ideas for the individual who holds them and believes in them. In fact, they have "kept her a practically well-woman for months after she should have given up and gone to bed," and they "have annulled all pain and weakness and given her a cheerful active life, unusually beneficial to others to whom she has afforded help."[77]

From this discussion on the power of ideas, James concludes that we humans possess powers of various kinds that we habitually fail to use, that in the employment of our basic mental faculties and mental coordination our lives "are contracted like the field of vision of an hysteric subject—but with less excuse, for the poor hysteric is diseased, while in the rest of us it is only an inveterate *habit*—the habit of inferiority to our full self—that is bad."[78]

Here, therefore, James circles back around to the problem he identified in "The Gospel of Relaxation," that we have developed bad habits as a result of our "imitation of bad models and the cultivation of false personal ideals."[79] Although he does not mention his earlier proposal that each of us, whatever our station in life, may become a positive model for others to imitate, he clearly considers the friend with breast cancer to be such a model for the simple reason that she beautifully exemplifies the power of ideas.

The Importance of the Individual

James concludes the address by returning to the issue with which he began: the fact that functional psychology has not been of much help in identifying the powers that we have available to us or the means by which we may unlock these reserves of power. He suggests, therefore, that some

77. Ibid., 1238.

78. Ibid., 1239. The "contraction" of the field of vision to which he has reference here is the inability of some hysterics to see or feel an object placed in front of them or pressed into their hands (James, *The Principles of Psychology*, 1:202–11).

79. James, "The Gospel of Relaxation," 832.

members of his audience might want to make this problem the object of their own research. Where these researches might go he does not profess to know, but he is certain that they would need to focus on the actual lives of individuals, for, however useful laboratory research may be, it cannot replicate the actual situations in which individuals find themselves, largely because it will never tax an individual's energies in ways as extreme as those forced upon them by the emergencies of life.[80] The British military officer during the siege of Delhi and the saintly friend with breast cancer are cases in point. Together, they illustrate the fact that these emergencies of life may be caused by internal threats (for example, cancer) as well as external ones (for example, war). Moreover, the case of James's European friend with the unstable nervous system indicates that constitutional or temperamental vulnerabilities may also tax an individual's energies in ways that laboratory research cannot begin to replicate. I will focus on the issue of temperamental vulnerabilities in chapter 7.

The Emancipated Mind and the Natural State of Dominant Calm

As I noted, James makes reference in "The Energies of Men" to Horace Fletcher's book *Happiness as Found in Forethought Minus Fearthought*. Fletcher wrote another book titled *Menticulture*, which James cites in his book *The Varieties of Religious Experience*.[81] Like Annie Payson Call, Fletcher makes an appeal in *Menticulture* to Nature. He notes that people have questioned his view, presented in his earlier book on happiness, that we should be able to get rid of our negative emotions and attitudes, and that, in raising these objections, they have invoked the fact that "in Nature there is sunshine and shadow, and that every height must have a corresponding depression." Therefore, they argue, "immunity from the black or shadowy passions is an unnatural condition."[82]

Fletcher disagrees with this argument by drawing attention to the process of growth and evolution of the natural world itself:

> In the process of growth and evolution, conditions that once were natural, are changed to other conditions equally natural. Weeds are pulled up by the roots to clear the field for the

80. James, "The Energies of Men," 1241.

81. James, *The Varieties of Religious Experience*, 181.

82. Fletcher, *Menticulture*, 34–35.

growing grain. Why should not mental weeds be pulled up by the roots also, and the mind cleared for growth? My experience teaches me that *the natural evolution of the emancipated mind is dominant calm,* varied by seasons of exaltation, but never of depression. It is a healthful succession of energy and rest, all blessed with loving appreciation, which finds expression in ever-present gratitude.[83]

On the other hand, one could argue that even fine old Nature herself has her bad days (not only lightning but also tornadoes, hurricanes, blinding snowstorms, and oppressive heat waves),[84] so it would not seem to be a sign of moral weakness were we at such times to invoke that other venerable imitative model that many of us learned about when we were children: I am referring here to Jesus and, specifically, to the occasion when he told his disciples to go into the boat and precede him to the other side of the lake while he dismissed the crowds to whom he had been speaking:

When evening came, he was there alone, but the boat by this time was many furlongs distant from the land, beaten by the waves; for the wind was against them. And in the fourth watch of the night he came to them, walking on the sea. But when the disciples saw him walking on the sea they were terrified, saying, "It is a ghost!" And they cried out in fear. But immediately he spoke to them, saying, "Take heart, it is I; have no fear." And Peter answered him, "Lord, if it is you, bid me come to you on the water." He said, "Come." So Peter got out of the boat and walked on the water and came to Jesus; but when he saw the wind, he was afraid and, beginning to sink, he cried out, "Lord, save me!" Jesus immediately reached out his hand and caught him, saying to him, "O man of little faith, why did you doubt?" And when they got into the boat, the wind ceased. And those in the boat

83. Ibid., 35 (italics added).

84. In *Menticulture* Fletcher tells about his experience as a boy of standing under a tree that was struck by lightning and receiving a shock. He notes that he "never knew exemption" from the effects of this experience "until I had dissolved partnership with worry. Since then lightning, and thunder, and storm clouds, with wind-swept torrents of rain have been encountered under conditions which formerly would have caused great depression and discomfort, without experiencing a trace of either" (34). In *Happiness as Found in Forethought Minus Fearthought,* Fletcher tells about how he helped some children and their mother overcome their fear of lightning and thunder by drawing attention to their beauty and their wonderful "big booms and bangs"(102).

worshipped him, saying, "Truly you are the Son of God" (Matt
14:22–33, RSV).

The implication, of course, is that even when fine old Nature is having
one of her bad days, we have nothing to fear because we have another
imitative model, one who has shown us that Nature cannot prevail over
us if our faith-thoughts are stronger than our fear-thoughts. But Fletcher
is also saying that Nature's good days far outweigh her bad days because
she is the very personification of *dominant* calm. So let nature be our
guide, and let her set our course. This means that when the mind avails
itself more fully of its available energies, it does not become frenetic or
agitated. Rather, the primary quality of the emancipated mind is one of
dominant calm, which manifests itself in a healthful alternation of energy
and rest, and in the release of enduring emotions of loving appreciation
and gratitude for life itself.

Conclusion

James does not make any direct references to older adults in either "The
Gospel of Relaxation" or "The Energies of Men." It is possible that the
woman he tells about in "The Energies of Men" who has been diagnosed
with breast cancer is an older woman, but James does not, in fact, indicate her age. Also, as I have noted, "The Gospel of Relaxation" is clearly
addressed to an audience of younger adults. But I believe that what James
has to say in these two addresses has particular relevance for older adults,
and that this is also true of what Annie Payson Call and Horace Fletcher
contribute to the discussion. After all, a relaxed body, an emancipated
mind, and the emotional state of dominant calm is a trinity that most
older adults desire and many have already achieved, thus serving as imitative models not only for other older adults but also for younger adults,
adolescents, and even children.

In fact, these acquisitions may well be a useful way of thinking and
talking about the wisdom of the old. If so, this may be wisdom that has
largely been acquired in their own older adult years as they have experienced unprecedented physical and mental vulnerabilities and discomforts, and the reality or anticipation of physical and mental suffering.[85]
As most older adults will attest, the realization of a relaxed body, an

85. I have addressed the latter in Capps, "Alzheimer's Disease and the Loss of Self."

emancipated mind, and a spirit of dominant calm is—or would be—no small achievement in this period of their lives.

Here, though, the cautionary note on which James concludes his address on the gospel of relaxation is especially relevant: He expresses the fear that "some one of my fair hearers may be making an undying resolve to become strenuously relaxed, cost what it will, for the remainder of her life."[86] This, however, is not the way to do it. Rather, "the way to do it, paradoxical as it may seem, is genuinely not to care whether you are doing it or not."[87] This not caring applies not only to the relaxation of the body but also to the emancipation of the mind and the spirit of dominant calm. And perhaps, whether we believe it or not, it is the older adult who is most favorably positioned *not* to care.

86. James, "The Gospel of Relaxation," 840.
87. Ibid.

7

Happy Spirits and Grumpy Souls

. . . . .

*Happy: having, showing, or causing a feeling of great
pleasure, contentment, joy, etc.*

Grumpy: grouchy, peevish, bad-tempered.

Self: the identity, character, or essential qualities of a person

Reconcile: to settle a quarrel, bring into harmony

. . . . .

FOLLOWING A CHAPTER BASED on the writings of a philosopher-psychologist, it may come as a welcome relief that this chapter focuses on a popular film—one that is neither mentally nor emotionally challenging. As I have already indicated, the film is Walt Disney's *Snow White and the Seven Dwarfs*. On the other hand, the topic of this chapter is no less serious than the topic of the preceding chapter, as it concerns the issue of mood and mood changes among older adults, and thus completes our discussion of the four dimensions of the experience of the aging process: body, mind, emotions, and moods.

Also, as I noted in the preceding chapter, this chapter will be concerned with the self, which the dictionary defines as "the identity, character, or essential qualities of any person or thing," and as "one's own person as distinct from all others."[1] I will be using the seven dwarfs as a metaphor for what Erik Erikson calls "the composite Self," which is made up of several selves.[2] This will enable us to consider the role of self-reconciliation in the growth and development that occurs in the aging process.

Mood Changes in Older Adulthood

Mood changes are not unique to older adults, but they seem to take on greater significance at this period in life. We notice them in other older adults and, if we are honest with ourselves, we also notice them in ourselves. They are typically unpredictable and often appear, at least to others, somewhat irrational. While there are usually external factors that precipitate such mood changes, the moods often seem to be out of proportion. Not all of these mood changes involve negative moods, for they can involve expressions of laughter and joy. But, generally speaking, they involve negative moods, such as irritability, anger, grouchiness, petulance, self-pity, or the like. Sometimes the mood change is brief and quickly passes. Other times it continues for hours, even a day or two. What causes this negative mood to lift is rather unpredictable, for even as the appearance of the mood tends to be disproportionate to the provocation, so its disappearance is difficult to account for.

In this chapter, I will be suggesting that such mood changes can be viewed more positively than is normally the case; that, in fact, they may be adaptive (as discussed in chapter 5) and, if recognized as such, treated with respect and even appreciation. I have chosen the alleged grumpiness of older persons, especially men, as illustrative.

To initiate this exploration, it will be useful to think of *moods* in relation to *emotions* on the one hand and *temperament* on the other. The dictionary defines *emotion* as "a strong feeling" and as "a state of consciousness having to do with the arousal of feelings, distinguished from other mental states, as cognition, volition, and awareness of physical sensation."[3] It defines *mood* as "a particular state of mind or feeling"

1. Ibid., 1300.
2. Erikson, *Identity, Youth, and Crisis,* 216–21.
3. Agnes et al., eds., *Webster's New World College Dictionary,* 466.

and as "a predominant or pervading feeling, spirit, or tone."[4] Thus, both *emotion* and *mood* have to do with feelings, but mood has the sense that the feelings are a pervasive state of mind. An *emotion* can be an enduring one, but it is more likely to come and go, perhaps in a matter of minutes or an hour or two at most. It may, of course, repeat itself over and over again until the situation that arouses it is finally resolved. In contrast, a *mood* may last for hours, days, or weeks. As it may not express itself strongly or dramatically, it may go unnoticed by others for quite a while, and even when others *do* notice it, they may not say anything about it in the belief—or hope—that it will soon pass and the other person will be his or her "normal" self again.

The dictionary defines *temperament* as "one's customary frame of mind or natural disposition" and makes a rather subtle distinction between *disposition* and *temperament* by noting that *disposition* "refers to the normal or prevailing aspect of one's nature (a genial disposition)" while *temperament* "refers to the balance of traits that are manifested in one's behavior or thinking."[5] An issue that especially interests me here is the potential impact of the mood changes that occur in older adulthood on one's *disposition* or *temperament*. A rather common observation made of certain older persons is that their temperament has changed: "He used to be so upbeat and full of life, but now he seems so downbeat and listless." Or, "She used to be so outgoing and friendly, but now she is withdrawn and impersonal." If moods are more enduring than emotions, they nonetheless have the connotation of being abnormal (we may say that a person seems "out of sorts today"). *Temperament*, though, has the sense of being fundamentally true of a person, or of being, in a sense, self-defining. We say, for example, that someone we know is "a happy person" or "a grumpy person," and the implication is that this is the person's basic or fundamental nature, and that everyone experiences this person in this way.

I am primarily concerned in this chapter with moods, especially in the sense that they reflect or express a predominant or pervading feeling,

4. Ibid., 935. This distinction between an emotion and a mood may well suggest that the "dominant calm" that we discussed in the preceding chapter should be viewed as a mood rather than as an emotion. In any case, in the context in which we were considering it, the important thing was that it signified an aspect of the individual that was distinguishable from ideas on the one hand (the mind) and behavior on the other (the body).

5. Agnes et al., eds., *Webster's New World College Dictionary*, 415.

spirit, or tone. But I am also concerned with temperament as the manifestation of the qualities or traits that compose one's personality, especially in those instances when one's temperament undergoes a significant change in older adulthood. Whether this change is one where a trait that was already a part of one's personality becomes more predominant in older adulthood or one where an entirely new trait appears is an interesting question, but it is not of primary concern here.

I have chosen to focus on two moods in this chapter: happiness and grumpiness. There are many other moods that I could have chosen instead. I believe, though, that there is a lot to be gained in our understanding of the role of moods in older adulthood by focusing on moods that are considered to be contrasting moods. Also, most everyone is able to recognize these moods and do not need special training in, for example, clinical psychology, to identify them. Furthermore, grumpiness is often attributed to older men.[6] Although such attributions may reflect ageism (an ageism that some older adults may share), I believe there is something to this attribution. That is, older persons—especially males—*do* seem to manifest a certain grumpiness. But a question I want to address here is whether this is always a bad thing. Are there not occasions when it is positively helpful or useful to be grumpy oneself or to have a grumpy soul around? I hope to make the case that there are such occasions.

If the focus here on grumpiness is rather easy to explain, the focus on happiness seems less so. After all, older adulthood is rarely referred to as the happiest period in one's life. In fact, the happiness factor may have played a significant role in the development of the iconic model of the life span that Paul W. Pruyser critiques (recall chapter 4), in which older adulthood is viewed as a period of decline. However, a primary reason for focusing on happiness is, as indicated above, that happiness is a mood that contrasts with grumpiness. It is not the only mood that contrasts with grumpiness—one could cite other contrasting moods such as cheerfulness, sanguineness, lightheartedness, and so forth—but a broader range of expressions and behaviors are associated with happiness. Another reason for choosing happiness is simply that I have coauthored a book on happiness, one that draws upon books written by experts on the subject.[7] I have learned from these experts that there are many different

6. See, for example, Prebble, *Grumpy Old Men*; Adams, *The Complete Geezer Guidebook*; and Wyer, *How Not to Murder Your Grumpy*; but also see Webber and Webber, *How To Become a Sweet Old Lady Instead of a Grumpy Old Grouch*.

7. Carlin and Capps, *100 Years of Happiness*.

avenues to happiness, and this very fact can be especially comforting to older adults who find that former avenues to happiness are no longer available or effective.

The title of this chapter refers to happy *spirits* and grumpy *souls*. This identification of the one as *spirits* and the other as *souls* is based on a discussion of the soul, spirit, and self in my book *A Time to Laugh*.[8] Spirit images are associated with light, rising, and ascendency while soul images are associated with darkness, depressions, and depths.[9] I noted that these associations are physically grounded because the early Israelites believed that the soul is located in the liver,[10] and the early Christians emphasized that the spirit is located in the heart. In this light, *happy* seems to be an expression of the spirit and *grumpy* seems to be an expression of the soul. (I suggested that the self has its locus in the brain because the brain is the seat of memory, which is essential to the individual's sense of being a self, for our sense of self-identity depends on our awareness of our having continuity over time.)

There are various ways that we might go about studying happy and grumpy moods, but I have chosen to focus here on the story of *Snow White and the Seven Dwarfs*. This is the story of how a princess stumbled onto the dwarfs' humble cottage when in flight from her stepmother, the wicked Queen, and found safety and sanctuary there.[11] Happy and Grumpy are two of the dwarfs. The others are Doc, Bashful, Sleepy, Sneezy, and Dopey. What makes Happy and Grumpy unique is that they form a pair because they are mirror images of each other. I will explore the implications of the special relationship between them in the course of this chapter.

8. Capps, *A Time to Laugh*, 104–12.

9. Hillman, *Re-visioning Psychology*, 68–69. See also Hillman, "Peaks and Vales."

10. See Jastrow, "The Liver as the Seat of the Soul"; and Selzer, *Mortal Lessons*, 63–68.

11. My personal associations with this story have less to do with having seen the 1937 Disney film at some point in my childhood and more to do with the fact that my dentist at the time gave children the seven dwarf figurines when a dental visit was concluded. Thus, this chapter has some direct associations with the article that Nathan Carlin and I wrote on the tooth fairy (see Donald Capps and Nathan Carlin, "The Tooth Fairy"). As a child I also referred to these figurines as "Dopeys," despite the fact that all seven dwarfs were included in the dentist's repertoire. This misnaming may have been due to the fact that Dopey was "the most successful and popular of the dwarf characterizations" (see *Wikipedia*, "Snow White and the Seven Dwarfs").

Mood, Temperament, Personality, and the Religious Sentiment

Before delving into the story of Happy and Grumpy, I would like to comment briefly on three sources that have informed my thinking about mood changes among older adults and the implications of these mood changes for our understanding of older adulthood. One is *Mood and Personality* by Alden E. Wessman and David F. Ricks.[12] As the title indicates, the authors focus on *mood* and its effect on personality. The dictionary indicates that the word *personality* is applied to "the sum of physical, mental, and emotional qualities that distinguish one as a person."[13] Thus, technically speaking, their study is not about *temperament*. But their chapters on the men and women they studied (all Harvard or Radcliffe students at the time) indirectly focus on temperament because they emphasize the predominant mood of the individual over time and changing circumstances. Thus, there is a chapter on the personality characteristics of a happy man and an unhappy man, and another chapter on the personality characteristics of a steady man and a moody man. Although Wessman and Ricks use the word *personality* to describe the characteristics of these men, it is quite apparent from their portrayals of the men that temperament is an important feature of their personalities. We might say that temperament is that feature of their personalities that is most attuned to their emotions and moods.

Another source that has informed my thinking on mood changes in older adulthood is an essay by Gordon W. Allport titled "What Units Shall We Employ?" in *Personality and Social Encounter*. This essay addresses the question: "What are the building blocks that comprise the edifice of a given personality?"[14] Among these building blocks, Allport identifies "syndromes of temperament," and notes that the efforts of various contemporary psychologists to shed light on the issue of temperament have enabled us to identify and assess "the prevailing 'emotional weather' in which personalities develop."[15] In focusing on happy spirits and grumpy souls I am concerned with identifying and assessing the prevailing emotional weather in which personalities tend to change over time as a consequence of the aging process itself.

12. Wessman and Ricks, *Mood and Personality*.
13. Agnes et al., eds., *Webster's New World College Dictionary*, 415.
14. Allport, "What Units Shall We Employ?," 111.
15. Ibid., 120.

Another source germane to the discussion here is Allport's introductory chapter of *The Individual and His Religion* on the origins of the religious quest.[16] Here he devotes a couple paragraphs to the role of temperament in the formation and maintenance of one's religious sentiment. He notes that some persons "live always close to the region of pain and melancholy [and] are bound to emphasize the grimmer aspects of whatever they encounter, and to stain their religious sentiment with their sense of forlornness," while others "have started in life with sparklets and bells [and] even in their moments of dependence they incline to take a sanguine view of the operations of Providence."[17] He adds:

> Both the gloomy and the gay may be concerned with the wrongness of life and may seek a religious mode of righting it, but their paths will be separate. Their theological and ritualistic preferences will differ according to their emotional thresholds, according to the quality of their prevailing mood, and according to their tendency to express or to inhibit feeling. Moreover, they are likely to be sharply biased in favor of these preferences, and correspondingly critical of others who find a different sort of religion better adapted to their needs. In this obdurate fact of temperament there lies a practical limitation to the aspirations of the current ecumenical movement.[18]

Allport adds in a footnote that he does not mean to suggest that the ecumenical movement is foredoomed to failure. After all, Roman Catholicism and Hinduism, which are both quasi-ecumenical, find room "for a great variety of temperaments." His point, rather, is that "it is difficult to write a formula for church unity in advance that will adequately respect the varieties of temperament seeking satisfaction in organized religion."[19]

Several aspects of Allport's account of the role of temperament in the formation and maintenance of one's religious sentiment are relevant to our exploration here. One is his observation that persons with a gloomy

16. Allport, *The Individual and His Religion*, 1–27.

17. Ibid., 12.

18. Ibid. The dictionary defines *gay* as "joyous and lively; merry; happy; lighthearted." It also defines *gay* as "homosexual (now often used specifically of male homosexuals)" (Agnes et al., eds., *Webster's New World College Dictionary*, 588). The former definition has fallen out of use, but I will retain Allport's original usage rather than employ a synonym because he clearly wanted to convey the opposite temperament of *gloomy*, which the dictionary defines as "very sad or dejected; hopeless; melancholy, morose or sullen" (ibid., 604).

19. Allport, *The Individual and His Religion*, 12.

and a gay temperament may both be concerned with the wrongness of life but their religious paths for righting the wrongs are different. Thus, it is not that the gloomy person is aware of the wrongness and the gay person is unaware of it. It is simply that they approach it differently. I will be making this case in relation to Happy (who has a gay temperament) and Grumpy (who has a gloomy temperament). Then, picking up on Allport's cautionary note about ecumenical efforts, I will suggest that if such unity remains elusive at the institutional level, perhaps it is achievable on the individual level. After all, Allport discusses the "integral nature of the mature sentiment" in his chapter titled "The Religion of Maturity."[20] Perhaps, therefore, Happy and Grumpy may live together in one's personality as complementary, and not merely as contrasting or conflicting, selves.[21]

The Creation of Happy and Grumpy

The two dwarfs Happy and Grumpy made their first appearance in the Disney film *Snow White and the Seven Dwarfs*.[22] The film was inspired by the story of Snow White, which is one of the eighty-six stories in the first edition of Jacob and Wilhelm Grimm's *Children's and Household Tales*, published in Germany in 1812, and commonly known as *Grimms' Fairy Tales*.[23]

In the original story the men that Snow White meets up with are simply referred to as seven woodsmen. They are not named. The naming of the seven woodsmen and their conceptualization as dwarfs[24] occurred

20. Ibid., 70–71.

21. My earlier discussion in chapter 2 of Erik H. Erikson's view that we are made up of various selves that compose our "composite Self" is relevant here. See Erikson, *Identity, Youth, and Crisis*, 216–21. I have also suggested in Capps, "Erik H. Erikson's Psychological Portrait of Jesus" that Jesus is the "self-reconciled one" (204–5). In effect, he personifies the integral nature of the religious sentiment. See also Erikson, "The Galilean Sayings and the Sense of 'I.'" I will return to the matter of self-reconciliation in the conclusion of this chapter.

22. Disney, *Snow White and the Seven Dwarfs*.

23. Grimm and Grimm, *The Complete Grimm's Fairy Tales*. See also *Wikipedia*, "Snow White and the Seven Dwarfs."

24. According to Agnes et al., eds., *Webster's New World College Dictionary*, the word *dwarf* refers to a member of a species (human, animal, plant) that is much smaller than the typical member of the species. It sometimes implies a malformation or disproportion of parts (444). For Disney's purposes, the representation of the seven

in the development of the Disney film, which was released on December 21, 1937.[25] This was the first feature film that Walt Disney produced. His wife, Lilian, and his brother Roy, who was also his business partner, tried to discourage him from making the film, and during its production the Hollywood movie industry referred to it as "Disney's Folly." He mortgaged his house to help finance the film's production, which eventually ran up a cost of nearly $1,500,000, a massive sum for a feature film in 1937. But the film was enormously successful and led the Disney studio to move ahead in the next two years with other feature-film productions, including *Pinocchio, Dumbo, Bambi, Alice in Wonderland,* and *Peter Pan.*

At the beginning of the project, Disney told his staff that the film's main attraction for him was the seven dwarfs and their possibilities for humor, especially visual gags such as the dwarfs' noses popping up at the foot of the bed when they first meet Snow White. Disney also wanted the film to begin with Snow White's discovery of the Cottage of the Seven Dwarfs and proposed that the dwarfs should have their own individual personalities. The dwarfs' names were chosen by the Disney staff from a pool of about fifty candidates, which included Jumpy, Deafy, Dizzy, Hickey, Wheezy, Baldy, Gabby, Nifty, Swift, Lazy, Puffy, Stuffy, Tubby, Shorty and Burpy. At an initial staff meeting five of the seven names were decided upon. These included Doc, Happy, Grumpy, Bashful, Sleepy, and Jumpy. Sneezy and Dopey were selected at a subsequent meeting and Jumpy was dropped from the list.[26]

When the film premiered on December 21, 1937, it received a standing ovation from a star-studded audience that included Charlie Chaplin, Judy Garland, Ginger Rogers, Jack Benny, Clark Gable, George Burns and Gracie Allen, Marlene Dietrich, and others. Six days later Walt Disney and the seven dwarfs appeared on the cover of *Time* magazine. By the end of the original run, the film had earned nearly eight million dollars. The film was rereleased in 1944 and on a regular cycle of every seven to ten

---

woodsmen as dwarfs afforded various comedic advantages. As the film was intended to appeal to children, their representation as dwarfs promoted children's self-identification with the dwarfs as a group, and one could also identify with a particular dwarf who manifested qualities that one recognized in oneself.

25. *Wikipedia,* "Snow White and the Seven Dwarfs."

26. I rather regret that Jumpy was dropped from the list because he would have afforded an interesting companion, temperamentally speaking, with Grumpy.

years thereafter. In commemoration of its fiftieth-anniversary release in 1987, Disney produced an authorized novelization of the story.[27]

Happiness and the Feeling of Satisfaction

In our book on happiness, Nathan Carlin and I have a section on some questions that have been raised about happiness. It includes chapters focusing on Ronald W. Dworkin's *Artificial Happiness* and Eric G. Wilson's *Against Happiness*.[28] Their inclusion in our book provides a cautionary note concerning happiness, namely, that it is all too easy to overlook the fact that happiness has its downside. To be sure, the chapters of our book that take a critical view of happiness are significantly outnumbered by the chapters that emphasize the positive aspects of happiness, but even these chapters raise questions concerning the dangers involved in over-idealizing happiness.

These cautionary notes are worth keeping in mind as we take a closer look at the two dwarfs—Happy and Grumpy—and make comparisons between them. It is worth noting in this regard that the *Wikipedia* article on the Disney film states that "Happy is the joyous dwarf and is usually portrayed laughing."[29] Given the fact that Snow White is being pursued by the wicked Queen who tricks her into biting a poisoned apple, which leads to her death, it could be argued that Happy personifies what Dworkin calls "the dark side" of the "happy class" and unintentionally supports Wilson's argument that there are times when melancholy is the more appropriate emotion. Of course, Disney does not present Happy as laughing when he and the other dwarfs discover that Snow White is dead. But the fact that he is named Happy raises the question whether there may be a myopic flaw in his outlook on the world due to a natural tendency to laugh.

Wessman and Ricks address this issue in their discussion of the case of a happy man they name Winn.[30] They preface their case of Winn with the observation that although readers might find themselves asking what he was trying to hide, their own answer to this question, based on three years of intensive study, would be that he was hiding very little, that to

---

27. Weyn, *Snow White and the Seven Dwarfs*.

28. Carlin and Capps, *100 Years of Happiness*, 145–87. See Dworkin, *Artificial Happiness*; and Wilson, *Against Happiness*.

29. *Wikipedia*, "Snow White and the Seven Dwarfs."

30. Wessman and Ricks, *Mood and Personality*, 145–69.

the best of their knowledge "Winn really was a happy man—a specimen rather rare in psychological literature."[31] On the other hand, they point out that "an element of over-control" runs through much of Winn's personal history: "His long-time steady girl, for example, accused him of thinking things through too much, never acting on impulse, and being too much the scientist in his everyday life."[32] The researchers attribute this element of over-control to the fact that Winn injured his younger brother Billy when he himself was six years old and Billy was three and a half. They were playing butcher, and Winn whacked Billy with a hatchet. The injury was not terribly serious, but it did require a couple of stitches. Moreover, Winn recalls that the incident "really scared my mother."[33]

The authors also note that Winn occasionally experienced mild depression, especially on days when he was physically ill, and that his mood would sometimes change from his customary warm and outgoing personality to "a more cautious position in which autonomy and resilience became more important than spontaneous social participation, and self-preoccupation replaced both warm human relationships and easy intellectual productivity."[34] On the other hand, because they were relatively rare, these occasional mood changes lent support to Wessman and Ricks's view that there were consistent themes in Winn's personality, including "a steadfast optimism, supported by independence and an active orientation toward the world, sociability and love of human contact, and a balance and maturity of judgment."[35]

The authors conclude their study of Winn with the observation that it has proven more difficult to explain Winn's happiness than the unhappiness of the person (Cage) who serves as Winn's counterpart. They think Winn was happy for several reasons: (1) there was a good fit between his personality and the existing American paths of upward mobility; (2) his optimism had been nurtured in a warm and admiring family circle; and (3) he had learned early in his life to control and delay his impulses in such a way that he reached the satisfactions he wanted with a maximum of dispatch and the provision of equal pleasure for the people around him.[36]

31. Ibid., 145.
32. Ibid., 152.
33. Ibid., 151.
34. Ibid., 166–67.
35. Ibid., 167.
36. Ibid., 168.

Wessman and Ricks suggest that "the old conception that happiness is the sum total of satisfactions minus the sum total of frustrations in a person's life" may be the best way to explain his happiness; but, if so, "Winn's successes were not of the calculating kind, and perhaps another source of his happiness was a reasonable willingness to accept limitations, to curb any inclinations he may have had toward narcissistic insatiability, and to tread the middle road between excess and deprivation with caution, intelligence, and due regard for his fellow man."[37]

Their conclusion that Winn was a genuinely happy man is supported by the dictionary definition of *happy* as "having, showing or causing a feeling of great pleasure, contentment, joy, etc."[38] Perhaps the key word here is *contentment*, for the dictionary defines *content* as "happy enough with what one has or is" and "not desiring something more or different; satisfied."[39] In contrast, the dictionary defines *grumpy* as "grouchy; peevish; bad-tempered,"[40] and the thesaurus identifies three synonyms for *grumpy—sullen, grouchy,* and *cantankerous—*that convey the sense or idea of grumbling, complaining, irritability and being hard to please.[41]

Thus, we might say that a key difference between Happy and Grumpy is that, temperamentally speaking, Happy is basically satisfied with things as they are, and, temperamentally speaking, Grumpy is not. Yet, even though it presents Happy in a much more positive light, perhaps this very difference allows us to make a certain case for Grumpy, and for taking a more sanguine view of the fact that Grumpy has become one of the selves that comprise one's composite Self. Conversely, the fact that, temperamentally speaking, Happy is basically satisfied with things as they are need not imply that he is unaware or oblivious to what Allport calls "the wrongness of life," or that he is any less likely to "seek a religious mode of righting it."[42] On the other hand, as Allport also notes, his temperament is likely to lead to a different path by way of addressing this wrongness. The wrongness in the case of *Snow White and the Seven Dwarfs* is, of course, the treatment of Snow White by the wicked Queen.

37. Ibid.

38. Agnes et al., eds., *Webster's New World College Dictionary*, 646.

39. Ibid., 314.

40. Ibid., 629.

41. Agnes et al., eds., *Webster's New World Roget's A-Z Thesaurus*, 354.

42. Allport, *The Individual and His Religion*, 12.

Grumpiness, Aging, and the Feeling of Dissatisfaction

In the following presentation of a case for Grumpy I will be quoting from the book *Snow White and the Seven Dwarfs* by Suzanne Weyn.[43] Published on the fiftieth anniversary of the film's release, Weyn's book is based on the film and was authorized by Disney himself. I assume that most readers know the story, but a brief summary of the story up to the point where Grumpy makes his appearance may be useful for those who do not.

Snow White lives in a grand castle, but her life is not carefree. Her kindhearted father is dead, and she has been left in the care of her wicked stepmother, the Queen. The Queen fears that someday Snow White's beauty will surpass her own, so she dresses the little princess in rags and forces her to work in the palace as a maid. Each day the Queen consults the Magic Mirror in a secret chamber in the palace and asks it to tell her who is the fairest in the land. It regularly assures her that she is the one. But in time her beauty fades, and the Mirror recognizes the beauty of Snow White, for the rags she is wearing "cannot hide her gentle grace."[44]

Then, one day, Snow White is down in the courtyard drawing water from the well. She doesn't really believe that the well is a magic wishing well but, just for fun, she leans forward and tells the well her dearest wish, that a handsome prince might come along and love her with all her heart. In fact, might it be today? Just then a handsome Prince is riding alongside the courtyard wall and hears her singing. He stops, and when he sees her dancing, his heart is filled with love.[45]

But the wicked Queen has witnessed their meeting from her high tower and resolves to get rid of Snow White. She commands a royal huntsman to take Snow White into the forest and find some secluded glen where she can pick some flowers. He immediately agrees. But then she adds, "And there you will kill her!"[46] He protests, but she says he undoubtedly knows the penalty if he should fail to carry out her command: the penalty is his own death. So he takes Snow White into the forest, but when he raises his knife to kill her, he begins to tremble and his knife falls to the ground. He can't do it. He tells her to run for her life because the Queen will stop at nothing to get rid of her, and when he returns to the

43. Weyn, *Snow White and the Seven Dwarfs*.
44. Ibid., 2.
45. Ibid., 4.
46. Ibid., 7.

castle, he tells the Queen he has carried out her command and gives her a pig's heart as proof that Snow White is dead.

Meanwhile, Snow White happens onto the humble cottage of the seven dwarfs and enters. They are not at home. They are at work in the magical jewel mine not far from their cottage. She is appalled by the awful mess she finds the cottage in, and drawing on her experience as a maid begins to clean it up, from top to bottom. She imagines that the inhabitants are orphans who don't have a mother, for a mother would never allow a cottage to become so filthy dirty. When she finishes cleaning she prepares a meal for the orphan children, then stretches out across three of the tiny beds she has discovered in a narrow little room and falls asleep.[47]

The encounter between the dwarfs and Snow White begins in chapter 5 of *Snow White and the Seven Dwarfs,* when the dwarfs return to their cottage after the day's work. They walk single file. Doc—described by the *Wikipedia* article on the making of the film as "pompous, self-important and bumbling"[48]—is in the lead. As they approach the cottage, they see that it is lit up, and they immediately became suspicious of foul play. So as they draw near to the cottage, they sneak up and peer through a window. When they do not see anyone inside, they enter by the front door. Doc warns the others to be careful and whispers, "Search every cook 'n' nanny—I mean hook 'n' granny, uh, crooked fan—I mean, search everywhere!"[49] As they search, they find that everything is spotlessly clean. Doc is greatly impressed, but Grumpy is not. The cleanliness of his little chair is evidence that "there's dirty work afoot," and he doesn't like this one bit: "He wanted his dirty old cottage back the way it was!"[50]

Happy responds very differently to these changes. When Sneezy observes that someone stole their dishes Happy tells him, "They ain't stole. They're here, hid in the cupboard." When Bashful lifts the lid of the heavy iron kettle and notes that "somethin's cooking," Happy says, "Smell's good" and grabs a clean spoon from the cupboard and runs toward the kettle. But Grumpy cries out, "Don't touch it, you fools! It might be poison," and just as he says the word "poison," the kettle lets off a burst of steam. "See," he says, "It's witches' brew."[51]

47. Ibid., 20.
48. *Wikipedia,* "Snow White and the Seven Dwarfs" (Wikipedia).
49. Weyn, *Snow White and the Seven Dwarfs,* 23.
50. Ibid., 26.
51. Ibid., 26–27.

Led by the twittering of birds in the rafters, the dwarfs climb up the stairs to the second floor to find and somehow evict the monster whom they believe has invaded their cottage. So when they enter the bedroom and see what they believe is the monster underneath the sheets, Grumpy says, "Let's attack while it's still sleeping."[52] The others think this is a good idea, but just as they are about to attack, Snow White begins to stir, and Doc pulls the sheet away and freezes in shock at the sight before him. "It's a girl!" he gasps. Sneezy declares, "She's mighty purty" and puts down his pickaxe, and Bashful agrees, "She beautiful—just like an angel." But Grumpy isn't going to be won over by this sleeping stranger: "Angel huh," he grumbles, "She's a female, an' all females is poison. They're fulla wicked wiles." Doc tells him to quiet down because he'd wake her. But Grumpy replies, "Aw—let her wake up. She don't belong here nohow."[53] Grumpy is right: Snow White does not belong here. Instead, she belongs in the castle at the top of the hill. On the other hand, she had not assumed an air of superiority when she entered their filthy cottage, but instead scrubbed and cleaned it and prepared a meal for them on their return. So it is true that she did not belong there, but it is also true that she had challenged the class structure that, under normal circumstances, would have made it highly unlikely that the dwarfs and the princess would meet and interact together.

When she identifies herself as a princess, Doc, in his rather bumbling way, says that they are greatly honored to have her in their little cottage. But Grumpy strongly disagrees. Honored? No way. "We're mad as hornets." He instructs Doc to "shut up and tell her to git out!" But Snow White begs them to allow her to stay because if they send her away, the Queen will kill her. The dwarfs had heard of the Queen's wicked ways, and Happy, "who usually thought well of everyone," declared, "She's bad." The others agreed with Happy—including Grumpy. But he felt that the very fact that the she was bad was grounds for sending Snow White away: "She's an old witch [but] I'm warnin' ya [that] if the Queen finds her here, she'll sweep down and get all of us."[54] When Snow White protests, "But she doesn't know where I am," Grumpy snorts, "She doesn't, eh? She knows everything. She's fulla black magic. She can make herself invisible." In fact, "She might be in this very room RIGHT NOW!"[55]

52. Ibid., 31.

53. Ibid., 32.

54. Ibid., 38.

55. Ibid., 39.

The other dwarfs briefly consider his argument, but Snow White says that her wicked stepmother will never find her here, and adds that if they let her stay, she will keep house, wash and sew, and sweep and cook for them. "Cook" was the magic word, for when she adds that she can make apple dumplings, plum pudding, and gooseberry pie, they shout "Hooray! She stays!"[56] Grumpy has been outvoted six to one.

Feeling empowered by the dwarfs' decision, Snow White insists that the dwarfs bathe in the tub before they can eat their dinner. All of the dwarfs protest, but eventually the others march outside where the tub is located, while Grumpy stands his ground. When Snow White asks him if he is going to wash, he won't answer her, and when she kindly asks him, "What's the matter? Cat got your tongue?" he sticks his tongue out at her. Then he turns his back on her and stomps off—crashing smack into the closed door. She smothers a giggle with her hand and asks, "Aw, did you hurt yourself?" Then she bends down to help the grouchy little fellow. He snorts at her and marches out to join the others in the yard.[57]

That evening, after they have eaten the sumptuous meal that Snow White had prepared for them, the dwarfs decide it was time for a party. They yodel and entertain Snow White with their instruments. Dopey beats a kettle drum, Sneezy and Bashful play concertinas, Sleepy blows into a little horn shaped like a fish, Happy strums a guitar-like instrument called a swanette, and Grumpy plays his finely carved organ. Doc approaches Snow White and makes a formal bow, prompting her to realize that she is being asked to dance. She hasn't had so much fun in many years.[58] After each of them had performed solo, Happy, not wanting the party to end, asks Snow White to perform, and when she asks what she should do, Sleepy asks her to tell a story because he always loves a good bedtime story before going to sleep. She proceeds to tell her own story of a princess who met a handsome prince and fell in love. Then, noticing that it has gotten late, she tells the dwarfs to go right up to bed, and as they are climbing the stairs, Doc stops the others and says that the princess will sleep in their own beds, and that they will sleep downstairs. Grumpy doesn't like this idea at all: "In a pig's eye," he grumbles.[59] Snow White looks at them and says, "Are you sure?" Happy says they'll be all

56. Ibid.
57. Ibid., 43–44.
58. Ibid., 48.
59. Ibid., 55.

right, and Doc tells her to go upstairs. They respond affirmatively when she asks if they will be comfortable downstairs. The minute she is gone, they dash around the cottage looking for a place to sleep. Grumpy ends up in a kettle and tosses and turns throughout the night. Upstairs, Snow White says her prayers and asks God to bless the dwarfs.[60]

But at this very time the wicked Queen is consulting her Magic Mirror. She asks, "Who now is the fairest of them all?" The Mirror replies, "In the cottage of the Seven Dwarfs dwells Snow White—fairest one of all."[61] Grumpy's warning to his fellow dwarfs has proven accurate. The wicked Queen will find Snow White, and their own lives will be in jeopardy. Initially, the Queen disputes with the Mirror: "Snow White lies dead in the forest. The huntsman has brought me proof. Behold her heart." But the Mirror replied, "Snow White still lives. 'Tis the heart of a pig you hold in your hand." She storms out of the room and descends the castle steps to the most ancient chambers of the castle, and here she formulates her plot to get rid of Snow White. In a shelf of ancient, dusty books she discovers a spell that will turn her own beauty into ugliness and change her queenly gowns into a peddler's cloak. She also finds a potion so cruel that it appeals to her evil nature. It is a poison apple that, when eaten, would produce a sleeping death. She also discovers that there is a cure—that the victim of the sleeping death can be awakened by love's first kiss—but she dismisses the idea that Snow White might survive. After all, when the dwarfs discovered Snow White, they would think she was dead and she would consequently be buried alive when they lowered her coffin into the ground.[62]

The wicked Queen comes to the dwarfs' cottage the next morning, after the dwarfs have gone to work, in the disguise of an old peddler woman. She entices Snow White to eat the poison apple by telling her that it is a Magic Wishing Apple and that with one single bite all of Snow White's dreams will come true. The forest animals are watching from the window and know that they must find the dwarfs and get them to return to the cottage. They catch up with the dwarfs just as the dwarfs are about to enter the mine. At first the dwarfs don't know what to think. They think the animals either are sick or have gone crazy. But finally Grumpy gets the message: "They ain't actin' this way for nothin',"

60. Ibid., 56–57.
61. Ibid., 48.
62. Ibid., 59.

and Sleepy shouts, "Maybe the old Queen's got Snow White!" Grumpy agrees, "The Queen will kill her! We've gotta save her." Doc replied, "Yes, but what'll we do?"[63] Grumpy jumps onto the back of one of the deer and motions the other dwarfs to follow him. At this very moment Snow White bites into the apple and she begins to feel dizzy. Suddenly she falls to the floor in a deep faint.

The Queen screams with laughter, declaring that she will now be the fairest in the land. But just as she says this, she hears the dwarfs dashing toward the cottage and runs out the front door. "There she goes!" cries Grumpy, who is the first to see her.[64] They chase her through the forest and in her panic she loses her way. Realizing she is trapped, she looks around and sees a rocky cliff. As she climbs up the cliff, the dwarfs scamper up the rocks after her. She screams at them, "I'll fix you. I'll crush your bones." As she speaks, she picks up the limb of a rotted tree and uses it to pry a large boulder loose.

Grumpy is the first to see what the witch is doing. "Look out!" he warns the others. Just then a bolt of lightning hits the edge of the cliff where the Queen is standing. The ledge shatters, throwing her over into the deep gorge below. The dwarfs run up to where she had been standing and look down. Below them is her dead body. They hurry back to their cottage and dash into the front room only to find Snow White on the floor, the poison apple still her in soft hands. Grumpy is the first to break into a loud sob: "We're too late," he wails, "Too late." The other dwarfs begin to cry, and the cottage is filled with weeping.

She is so beautiful, even in death, that the dwarfs cannot find it in their hearts to bury her. They build a coffin not of wood but of glass and gold, and they keep watch over her day and night. The prince hears that a young maiden has died and lies in a glass coffin, and he soon comes to the dwarfs' cottage. He kneels by her side and kisses her, and she begins to move. When she opens her eyes and sees the prince, she reaches out to him, and he quickly sweeps her up in his arms. The dwarfs yell with joy. Doc and Grumpy hug one another, and Happy and Sneezy throw their hats in the air. Snow White kisses each of the dwarfs joyfully, and the prince carries her to his horse. She waves goodbye to the dwarfs as she

63. Ibid., 66.
64. Ibid., 69.

lets him lead her out of the forest and toward his own castle where they live happily ever after.[65]

The reader of *Snow White and the Seven Dwarfs* cannot miss the fact that Grumpy plays a central role in the events that follow the night of the party, which leads, in turn, to the new sleeping arrangement in the cottage. This role flows from Grumpy's natural disposition to be alert to the fact that things can go seriously wrong in the world he inhabits. Thus, when the animals appear to others to be sick or crazy, he takes their strange behavior to be evidence of the fact that something is terribly wrong. Grumpy is not the first to intuit that the Queen may be up to something; the honor here goes to Sleepy, the dwarf who is described in the *Wikipedia* article on the making of the film as appearing "laconic in most situations."[66] But perhaps it is precisely because he has so little to say that Grumpy takes Sleepy seriously and immediately agrees with him. Not only that, but Grumpy believed that the Queen was capable of the worst thing imaginable: killing Snow White. And whereas the dwarfs' leader, Doc, seems immobilized at this point, Grumpy acts quickly, and it is he who leads the charge to save the princess.

Grumpy as an Older Adult

While there are obvious reasons for viewing Grumpy as a young or middle adult (for example, the fact that he and his fellow dwarfs are setting off for work every day) and not an older adult, I have found it quite illuminating to imagine him as being the prototypical grumpy old man. When one does take this imaginative leap, one notices that he possesses several qualities that grumpy old men tend to manifest. It would not be at all difficult to view Grumpy as the prototypical grumpy old man. For example, at the beginning of the story he is the one who does not like the fact that Snow White has made the cottage spotlessly clean. We might say that here he is manifesting the characteristic of the grumpy old man to oppose change even if the change is clearly for the betterment of everyone—including Grumpy himself—affected by it. Or when Grumpy contends that Snow White doesn't belong in the cottage occupied by the dwarfs, we might say that he was manifesting another characteristic of

65. Ibid., 73.
66. *Wikipedia*, "Snow White and the Seven Dwarfs."

the grumpy old man to insist on rigid rules as to who belongs and who doesn't belong.

We might also see in his argument that Snow White's wicked stepmother is probably already aware that Snow White is staying in their cottage the ability of the grumpy old man to perceive real dangers that others consider highly improbable, plus the tendency not to persist when others reject his warnings and perhaps to grouse to himself that *they will find out that I was right*. We might also see in Grumpy's response to Snow White's insistence that the dwarfs bathe in the tub before they eat their dinner the tendency of the grumpy old man to refuse to get with the program and, in doing so, to behave in ways that are self-demeaning.

But if Grumpy fits the overwhelmingly negative image of the grumpy old man, he seems also to redeem himself when he perceives the danger that Snow White is in and immediately takes charge. We do not ordinarily think of older persons as moving quickly and taking charge. On the contrary, they are viewed as slow and indecisive. But might this not be a stereotype? Or perhaps it is generally true when the stakes are low and the older person, on the basis of years of experience, lets those who are younger muddle their way through an issue or problem, perhaps recalling when he or she did the same. But in this case the stakes are high, and I have to say that in this situation I would trust Grumpy more than I would Doc, the official leader; or Happy, the fellow who seems aware of the problem but does not offer a solution.

Something else going on here with Grumpy that can also be true of the older person, although we do not normally perceive it, is the fact that Grumpy has come full circle as far as Snow White and her fate are concerned. Initially, he disagrees with the idea of inviting her to live with the dwarfs in their humble cottage, because her presence could place them all in jeopardy. He seems at that point to accept the possibility, even the likelihood, that if they do not invite her to stay, she will be killed by the wicked Queen. Grumpy bases his acceptance of this possibility on the fact (which is true) that she does not belong there. In fact, the story ends with Snow White taking up residence in the Prince's castle. But by the end of the story Grumpy has completely changed his mind about Snow White.

The morning after the party when the dwarfs set off for work, there is a sense of foreboding in the air. Doc is the first to leave the house, and as he does so, he warns Snow White, "Don't forget, my dear, the—the old Queen is a sly one. She's fulla witchcraft."

She tells him not to worry, and kisses him on the forehead. Bashful stammers a similar note of caution, and she kisses him too. Grumpy is the last to leave the house. He marches past Snow White without a word, but then he turns back and says, "Now I'm warnin' ya. Don't let nobody or nothin' in the house."

"Oh, Grumpy, you do care!" cries Snow White happily, and she kisses him too. He breaks away from her and runs. But when he was sure no one could see him, "he smiled and breathed a sigh of pleasure."[67] Snow White had won him over. And perhaps this is yet another quality of the grumpy old man—and of his female counterpart—that we tend to overlook. It's easy to say that older persons are "set in their ways" and for older persons themselves to agree with this view, especially with regard to other older adults. But if so, this makes the occasions when they *do* change all the more noteworthy and, in the case of Grumpy's feelings toward Snow White, truly heartwarming as well. Moreover, his actions following his realization that the animals are trying to warn them are proof that the change in him is both real and deep. As Snow White sees, he genuinely cares for her, and it is doubtful that she would have survived had he not taken the initiatives that he took in her behalf.

This is not, of course, to idealize Grumpy. Much of the time the characteristics of Grumpy are irritating to those who have to live with him; and, if he could admit it, he finds them irritating to himself as well. But a significant difference between Grumpy and Happy—at least in the story—is that Happy has a tendency to accept things as they are, and Grumpy does not. Perhaps this difference is what Allport has in mind when he suggests that persons of gay and gloomy temperaments recognize the wrongness in life but respond in different ways: for example, the gay temperament more inclined than the gloomy temperament to trust in a transcendent intervention. In any event, Grumpy rejects the very idea that a Queen who wants to put an end to Snow White, the woman who is destined to be the Prince's wife, will prevail. This simply cannot be.

To be sure, Grumpy is not the one who eventually brings Snow White back from her sleeping death. This is the Prince's task. But he uses the power that he possesses to create the conditions that make it possible for the Prince to restore her to life and enable her to live happily ever after. Happiness, then, is very much to be desired, but sometimes a grumpy soul is needed to bring it about.

67. Weyn, *Snow White and the Seven Dwarfs*, 62.

The Ecumenical *I* and Self-Reconciliation

In conclusion, I would suggest that the grumpy soul may be a rather late temperamental addition to the personality that has been of a predominantly happy temperament, and I have attributed this addition in some cases (my own included) to the aging process. In taking this view, I am aware of the fact that I am endorsing the popular view that the grumpy temperament may well be disproportionately found among older men. It would probably have been easier and certainly more convenient simply to dispute—even protest—this popular view. Instead, I have accepted its essential truth but have set about to make a positive case for the grumpy soul. I would not have accepted its essential truth or have made a case for the grumpy soul if I believed that grumpy old men are nothing but grumpy souls. Instead, I am convinced that Grumpy is only one of the seven dwarfs that inhabit the cottage that I know as myself, and, this being the case, he must share the living space with Doc, Happy, Bashful, Sneezy, Sleepy, and Dopey.

Thus, to invoke Gordon Allport's image of the ecumenical movement in reference to the role of temperament in the formation and maintenance of the religious sentiment, I want to suggest that the "composite Self" that Erik H. Erikson discusses in *Identity, Youth, and Crisis* is itself an ecumenical body composed of various selves. As I noted in chapter 2 (and in footnote 21 of the present chapter), Erikson suggests that the *I* is composed of various selves that together make up our "composite Self." Observing that each of these selves reflects one's experience of various and distinctive psychosocial conditions, he adds, "It takes, indeed, a healthy personality for the 'I' to be able to speak out of all these conditions in such a way that at any given moment it can testify to a reasonably coherent Self."[68]

I myself would want to testify to the fact that for some of us older adults there is a special bond between Happy and Grumpy—one that is reflective of the unity that the religious sentiment espouses—because they have a similar outlook on the world but choose to relate to it differently. Happy tries to adapt as best he can to the "wrongness in life," and Grumpy feels the need to complain and, if possible, to do something about it.[69]

68. Erikson, *Identity, Youth, and Crisis,* 217.

69. This is not to say that what Grumpy does will always be the right thing, nor does it mean that his efforts will always be effective or successful. In this regard, his

On the other hand, the ultimate goal of the healthy personality is to sustain a sense of camaraderie between the *several* selves that constitute the composite Self or sense of *I*. In the story of *Snow White and the Seven Dwarfs* this camaraderie is palpably evident during the party that follows the sumptuous meal that Snow White had prepared for the seven dwarfs: each of them took his turn in entertaining the others. Even Bashful sang a little song.[70] Their performances were far from perfect, but that's beside the point. What mattered is that they were manifesting the fact that they truly belonged to one another precisely because they had different qualities and capacities. As we have seen, Grumpy is the one among them who could be counted upon to do everything within his power to challenge the forces in this world determined to separate one from another. After all, he and not their titular leader Doc was the one who led their successful charge against the wicked Queen.

Then, of course, there are the internal forces, dementia chief among them, that threaten the very existence of the composite Self. There is not much we can do about this unholy harbinger of death itself when it comes knocking on our door.[71] But I believe that older adulthood affords a golden opportunity to settle preexisting quarrels and conflicts between the various selves that make up our composite Self. As we saw in chapter 3, Erik Erikson ascribes the quality of integrity to older adulthood, and in this regard he emphasizes the individual's "proclivity for order and meaning."[72] There are various ways this proclivity is expressed, but the reconciliation of the various selves that make up our "composite Self" is certainly one of them. Moreover, we may view this reconciliation of our various selves as a reflection of the religious sentiment that Gordon Allport describes in *The Individual and His Religion*. He writes:

---

actions in saving Snow White may serve the common, ordinary Grumpy as a model of exemplary action, as an ideal to aspire to, and it is significant in this regard that he doesn't try to do it all himself but elicits the assistance of his comrades. There are also situations in which taking any action at all would be fruitless, and it is here that Grumpy would do well to emulate Happy and, as the saying goes, learn to "grin and bear it."

70. If I had written about *Snow White and the Seven Dwarfs* in my young adulthood or middle adulthood, I am quite certain that I would have focused on Bashful rather than Happy and Grumpy. See Capps, *Social Phobia*. This, however, illustrates the fact that we tend to privilege different expressions of our composite Self at different stages of life.

71. See Capps, "Alzheimer's Disease and the Loss of the Self."

72. Erikson, *Childhood and Society* (1st ed.), 232.

Psychology's chief contribution to mental health is the concept
of integration, a term less Biblical, but meaning much the same
as St. James's "single-mindedness" [James 1:8]. Integration
means the forging of approximate mental unity out of discor-
dant impulses and aspirations. No one can say, "I will integrate
my life," and expect to find it done. For the most part integration
is a by-product of various favorable techniques of living. Perfect
integration, of course, is never achieved, but to be reasonably
successful it must, as we have seen, admit the requirements of
the mature conscience. All strongly ideal interests, we know,
tend to unify the mind. But in principle, the religious interest,
being most comprehensive, is best able to serve as an integrative
agent.[73]

This integration—what I have been referring to as self-reconciliation—
may be the most significant of all expressions of creativity in older
adulthood.

A Final Word on the Subject of Moods

Throughout this chapter I have been operating on the assumption that
mood changes, including ones generally considered negative, are an inevitable feature of older adulthood, and this being the case, I wanted to
defend the grumpy mood often ascribed to older men. However, what
I have not considered here is the possibility that such moods might be
completely eradicated. This possibility is explored by Annie Payson Call,
whom we met in chapter 6, in her chapter on moods in *As a Matter of
Course*.[74]

She suggests that a useful method for ridding oneself of a bad mood
is to realize their superficiality. She explains:

> Moods are deadly, desperately serious things when taken seri-
> ously and indulged in to the full extent of their power. They are
> like a tiny spot directly in front of the eye. We see that and that
> only. It blurs and shuts out everything else. We groan and suffer
> and are unhappy and wretched, still persistently keeping our eye
> on the spot, until finally we forget that there is anything else in
> the world. In mind and body we are impressed by that and that
> alone. Thus the difficulty of moving off a little distance is greatly

73. Allport, *The Individual and His Religion*, 91.

74. Call, *As a Matter of Course*, 30–33.

increased, and liberation is impossible until we do move away, and, by a change of perspective, see the spot for what it really is.[75]

One change of perspective that can be useful is to take a good look at all past moody states, for, in doing so, one will immediately realize that "they come from nothing, go to nothing, and are nothing." Then, when the mood reappears, one can declare that this *is* a mood and challenge it to do its worst because "I can stand it as long as you can." Thus challenged, the mood dissolves for want of nourishment. Another useful method is to think of a mood as similar to a person who enjoys teasing others. As Call points out,

> It is well known that the more we are annoyed, the more our opponent teases; and that the surest and quickest way of freeing ourselves is not to be teased. We can ignore the teaser externally with an internal irritation which he sees as clearly as if we expressed it. We can laugh in such a way that every sound of our own voice proclaims the annoyance we are trying to hide. It is when we take his words for what they are worth, and go with him, that the wind is taken out of his sails, and he stops because there is no fun in it. The experience with a mood is quite parallel, though rather more difficult at first, for there is no enemy like the enemies in one's self, no teasing like the teasing from one's self. It takes a little longer, a little heartier and more persistent process of non-resistance to cure the teasing from one's own nature. But the process is just as certain, and the freedom greater in result.[76]

Call suggests that this process of nonresistance and its therapeutic effects is expressed in these words of Jesus: "If a man takes your cloak, give him your coat also; if one compels you to go a mile, go with him two" (Matt 5:41); "Love your enemies, do good to them that hurt you, and pray for them that despitefully use you" (Matt 5:44). She asks:

> Why have we been so long in realizing the practical, I might say the physiological, truth of this great philosophy? Possibly because in forgiving our enemies we have been so impressed with the idea that it was our enemies we were forgiving. If we realized that following this philosophy would bring us real freedom, it would be followed steadily as a matter of course, and with no more sense that we deserved credit for doing a good

75. Ibid., 30–31.
76. Ibid., 31.

thing than a man might have in walking out of prison when his
jailer opened the door. So it is with our enemies the moods.[77]

Call concludes that it is when we exaggerate the seriousness of moods
that they lose their power for good and make slaves of us.

Hopefully, by focusing here on the two dwarfs Happy and Grumpy
our own reflections on moods avoid the danger of taking our moods
too seriously and thereby allowing them to become our masters. And
perhaps our focus on Grumpy especially will help us to be tolerant of
others who manifest moods of grumpiness, irritability, or self-pity. As
Call points out:

> As we gain freedom from our own moods, we are enabled
> to respect those of others and give up any endeavor to force
> a friend out of his moods, or even to lead him out, unless he
> shows a desire to be led. Nor do we rejoice fully in the extreme
> of his happy moods, knowing the certain reaction. Respect for
> the moods of others is necessary to a perfect freedom from our
> own. In one sense no man is alone in the world; in another sense
> every man is alone; and with moods especially, a man must be
> left to work out his own salvation, unless he asks for help. So, as
> he understands his moods, and frees himself from their mas-
> tery, he will find that moods are in reality one of Nature's gifts, a
> sort of melody which strengthens the harmony of life and gives
> it a fuller tone. Freedom from moods does not mean the loss
> of them, any more than non-resistance means allowing them
> to master you. It is non-resistance, with the full recognition of
> what they are, that clears the way.[78]

I can see Happy and Grumpy nodding to themselves—and one
another—in wholehearted agreement with Annie Payson Call. And, as
far as I can tell, I am seeing clearly—no tiny spot, speck, or log (Matt
7:3)—but just a simple vision of a couple of dwarfs who are doing their
best to get along with each other and, what's more, finding that they truly
enjoy each other's company.

77. Ibid., 32. Note her use here of the title of her book: As a Matter of Course.
78. Ibid., 33.

EPILOGUE

Aging Horses and Wounded Healers

. . . . .

Aging: to grow old or show signs of growing old

Wounded: an injury caused by an external force

. . . . .

IT SHOULD BE CLEAR from the previous chapters that this is not a book
about ministering to older adults. If anything, it is a book that challenges
the idea that older adults are in any greater need of ministry than middle
or young adults. However, as my own autobiographical reflections in
chapter 2 suggest, there are times when an older adult welcomes the companionship of a younger person in the journey described in chapter 4.

This brief epilogue is therefore intended for those who have chosen
to become ministers and whose responsibilities include providing companionship and other forms of assistance to older adults. It reflects the
fact that prior to my official retirement, I regularly taught a course titled
Poetry and the Care of Souls. From teaching this course I have learned
that poems about dogs outnumber poems about horses by about one
hundred to one. Many of our major contemporary poets have written
poems about dogs, and there are whole books of poems about dogs.[1] Po-

---

1. See, for example, Hempel and Shephard, eds., *Unleashed: Poems by Writers'
Dogs*; and Duemer and Simmerman, eds., *Dog Music: Poetry about Dogs*.

ems about horses, though, are relatively rare. The logical explanation for this is that dogs are far more common than horses. If one were to see a horse rambling through town these days, one would assume that something is amiss. Not so with a dog. In fact, dogs are such a common sight in the world in which we humans live that we often take their presence for granted.[2]

But when I considered the few poems on horses with which I was acquainted, a subtle, deeper explanation presented itself. This is the fact that horses are associated with aging. Some of us recall the popular song, "The Old Grey Mare, She Ain't What She Used to Be," which suggests that she was quite impressive "many long years ago," but, alas, not any more.

Two poems illustrate the point that horses are associated with aging; when viewed as a team, so to speak, they also illustrate the vicissitudes of aging. Here is a poem by Jane Kenyon, who died of leukemia at the age of forty-eight. It was inspired by her husband's mother.[3]

In the Nursing Home

She is like a horse grazing
a hill pasture that someone makes
smaller by coming every night
to pull the fences in and in.
She has stopped running wide loops,
stopped even the tight circles.
She drops her head to feed; grass
is dust, and the creek bed's dry.
Master, come with your light
halter. Come and bring her in.

This poem, which is about an older woman who has no prospects of returning to her own home, emphasizes the fact that her living space has

---

2. I had a dream, around the time that I was retiring from my faculty position at Princeton Theological Seminary, in which a dog came out of a house and joined me as I was walking up the street. He accompanied me awhile, and then I became concerned that he might not be able to find his way home, so I suggested to him that he should probably start back. He looked at me and then looked back at the house from which he had emerged and said, in a wistful tone of voice, "Sometimes those who make the decisions are not the wisest ones." I have some guesses as to the meaning of the dream, which are not really relevant here, but I would like to note that I felt his companionship and wished that we could have continued on our journey together.

3. Kenyon, *Collected Poems*, 282. See Timmerman, *Jane Kenyon*, 220–21.

become very constricted. Moreover, her life consists of eating a bit, but of little else. It seems merciful, therefore, that the "Master" would come with his light halter and "bring her in." Here, the horse serves as a metaphor for old age, and for that time when we humans are, quite literally, on our last legs.

But here is a poem that takes a rather different, if complementary, view of the aging process: the poet is William Stafford, and the poem was originally published in 1992, when Stafford was sixty-eight years old. He lived to age seventy-nine.[4]

A Few Snorts from a Wild One

Life sleeps in this tired old horse, but might
wake yet for a spur or a fire when the muscles
come alive, till even the main gate creaks
as a shoulder hits it and makes the whole corral
shudder its rails while its weakest post
almost gives way. Some time it will, maybe
tomorrow; and then you'll see: I guarantee you
the road out of here will be filled with a horse.

In this poem about an older person, the horse is in the corral and spends a good bit of his time sleeping. But some stimulus—a spur to its flanks, or a fire—may arouse him, and once aroused, this old horse is altogether likely to flex his muscles, break through the main gate, and rip-snort his way out into the road. When will this happen? Although no one—himself included—really knows, it *could* be as early as tomorrow. In any case, the poet "guarantee[s]" that it will, in fact, occur.

Thus, in these two poems we have two images of the aging horse: In the first, the horse, reduced to walking in smaller and smaller circles, is at last brought in by the Master, and her grazing days are over. In the second, the horse, confined to a corral, has one last burst of energy reminiscent of his early days as a wild one. Both images are true, and together, they express the vicissitudes of growing old.

Those who are growing old have little difficulty recognizing the truth of these poems. But what about those who are younger, those who may be offering a helping hand to the older persons in their home congregations, retirement communities, nursing homes, hospitals or hospice centers? Although it may seem that these younger persons have little in

4. Stafford, *The Way It Is*, 23.

common with the older ones, a poem by Denise Levertov suggests otherwise. This poem was originally published in 1967, when Levertov was forty-four years old.[5]

Bedtime

We are a meadow where the bees hum,
mind and body are almost one
as the fire snaps in the stove
and our eyes close
and mouth to mouth, the covers
pulled over our shoulders,
we drowse as horses drowse afield,
in accord; though the fall cold
surrounds our warm bed, and though
by day we are singular and often lonely.

This poem makes an observation about horses that Kenyon's poem does not, namely, that if horses in the field graze separately, they usually doze off together. As one walks down the hall of the nursing home in the afternoons and at night, one may listen for the collective snoring of the residents. As Stafford puts it, "Life sleeps in this tired old horse."

But Levertov makes another observation that encourages us to consider what those who are younger and engaged in ministry to the older ones have in common with them. This is the simple fact of their shared loneliness. In *The Wounded Healer*, Henri Nouwen suggests that the minister is called "not only to care for his own wounds and the wounds of others, but also to make his wounds into a major source of his healing power."[6] Then he asks:

But what are our wounds? They have been spoken about in many ways by many voices. Words such as "alienation," "separation," "isolation" and "loneliness" have been used as names of our wounded condition. Maybe the word "loneliness" best expresses our immediate experience and therefore most fittingly enables us to understand our brokenness. The loneliness of the minister is especially painful; for over and above his experience as a man

---

5. Levertov, *Selected Poems*, 66.
6. Nouwen, *The Wounded Healer*, 82–83.

in modern society, he feels an added loneliness, resulting from the changing meaning of the ministerial profession itself.[7]

Concerning the professional loneliness of the minister, Nouwen notes that "the painful irony is that the minister, who wants to touch the center of men's lives, finds himself on the periphery, often pleading in vain for admission. He never seems to be where the action is, where the plans are made and the strategies are discussed."[8] Nouwen adds:

> The wound of our loneliness is indeed deep. Maybe we had forgotten it, since there were so many distractions. But our failure to change the world with our good intentions and sincere actions and our undesired displacement to the edges of life have made us aware that the wound is still there. So we see how loneliness is the minister's wound not only because he shares in the human condition, but also because of the unique predicament of his profession. It is this wound that he is called to bind with more care and attention than others usually do. For a deep understanding of his own pain makes it possible for him to convert his weakness into strength and to offer his own experience as a source of healing.[9]

One could read these quotations from Nouwen as descriptions of not only the minister but also the older adult—on the periphery, not where the action is, excluded from the planning and the strategizing, unsuccessful in earlier efforts to change the world with good intentions and sincere actions, and displaced to the edges of life. Perhaps, then, the conclusion to draw is that ministers, whatever their personal, chronological age, are, professionally speaking, old beyond their years.[10] And this, we might say, is their peculiar strength.

7. Ibid., 83.

8. Ibid., 86.

9. Ibid., 87. See also Day, *The Long Loneliness.*

10. Younger ministers' recognition of the fact that they share a sense of loneliness in common with older adults may also work against the tendency of younger persons to have negative views of and attitudes toward older persons because older persons represent to those who are younger the threat that they will experience the same fate at some future time. In other words, if younger persons and older persons share an important characteristic or quality in common in the here and now, there may be less likelihood that the younger persons will see older persons as merely representing the *future,* one that the younger person reacts against. See Greenberg et al., "Aging."

Loneliness and Creativity

As I suggested in the concluding paragraph of the introduction, we may view God as the original Creative Self. This means that the creative self in older adulthood has its ultimate basis in the fact that we are created in the very image of God. This fact, together with the fact that loneliness may well be the basis for younger ministers' recognition of themselves in older adults, indicates that there is a profound relationship between loneliness and creativity. As James Weldon Johnson (1871–1938), the African American songwriter, American consul to Venezuela and Nicaragua, executive secretary of the NAACP, and professor of creative literature at Fisk University, suggests in his poem "The Creation," God created the world out of a deep sense of personal loneliness.[11] The poem begins:

> And God stepped out on space
> And he looked around and said:
> I'm lonely—
> I'll make me a world.
>
> And as far as the eye of God could see
> Darkness covered everything,
> Blacker than a hundred midnights
> Down in a cypress swamp.
>
> Then God smiled,
> And the light broke,
> And the darkness rolled up on one side,
> And the light stood shining on the other,
> And God said: "That's good!"

God went on to make the sun, the moon, and the earth, and seeing that the earth was hot and barren, he sent the cooling waters, which led the green grass to sprout and the little red flowers to blossom. They were followed by the creation of fishes and fowls, and beasts and birds who roamed the forests and the woods, and split the air with their wings. Seeing what he had made, God said: "That's good!"

But as he walked around, and looked on his world with all its living things, he said, "I'm lonely still." So he sat down on the side of a hill where he could think:

---

11. Johnson, *God's Trombones*, 17–20

By a deep, wide river he sat down;
With his head in his hands,
God thought and thought: I'll make me a man!

Up from the bed of the river
God scooped the clay;
And by the bank of the river
He kneeled him down;
And there the great God Almighty
Who lit the sun and fixed it in the sky,
Who flung the stars to the most far corner of the night,
Who rounded the earth in the middle of his hand;
This Great God,
Like a mammy bending over her baby,
Kneeled down in the dust
Toiling over a lump of clay
Till he shaped it in his own image;

Then into it he blew the breath of life,
And man became a living soul.
Amen. Amen.

We say that God created the world out of nothing, but perhaps it would
be more accurate to say that God created the world—and created us—
out of a deep sense of loneliness. And perhaps this means that a similar
sense of loneliness in this world that we inhabit is, for us, the underlying
inspiration for our own creativity. And maybe it is the older adult who is
especially aware that this is so.

Permissions

Billy Collins, "Flames" from *The Apple That Astonished Paris*. Copyright © 1988, 1996 by Billy Collins. Reprinted with permission of The Permissions Company Inc. on behalf of the University of Arkansas Press, www.uapress.com.

Jane Kenyon, "In the Nursing Home" from *Collected Poems*. Copyright © 2005 by The Estate of Jane Kenyon. Reprinted with the permission of The Permissions Company Inc. on behalf of Graywolf Press, Minneapolis, Minnesota, www.graywolfpress.org.

Denise Levertov, from *Poems 1960–1967*, copyright © 1966 Denise Levertov. Reprinted by permission of New Directions Publishing Corp.

William Stafford, "A Few Snorts from a Wild One" from *The Way It Is: New and Selected Poems*. Copyright © 1962, 1977, 1998 by William Stafford and the Estate of William Stafford. Reprinted with permission of The Permissions Company, Inc. on behalf of Graywolf Press, Minneapolis, Minnesota, www.graywolfpress.org

"Touch Me." Copyright © 1995 by Stanley Kunitz, from *The Collected Poems*, by Stanley Kunitz. Used by permission of W. W. Norton & Company Inc.

From Springer Publications:

Donald Capps, "Fired Up and Loaded For Bear," *Pastoral Psychology* 59 (2010) 671–77.*

Donald Capps, "An Overdue Reunion," *Pastoral Psychology* 60 (2011) 167–77.

Donald Capps, "Relaxed Bodies, Emancipated Minds, and Dominant Calm," *Journal of Religion and Health* 48 (2009) 368–80.*

Donald Capps, "Happy Spirits and Grumpy Souls: Mood Changes in Older Adulthood," *Pastoral Psychology* (2013) published online.

From Journal Editor:

Donald Capps, "Aging Horses and Wounded Healers," *Journal of Pastoral Care and Counseling* 62 (2008) 293–96.

Bibliography

Adams, Charles F. *The Complete Geezer Guidebook: Everything You Need to Know about Being Old and Grumpy.* Fresno, CA: Quill Driver, 2009.

Agnes, Michael, et al., eds. *Webster's New World College Dictionary.* Foster City, CA: IDG Books Worldwide, 2001.

———, eds. *Webster's New World Roget's A–Z Thesaurus.* Cleveland: Wiley, 1999.

Allport, Gordon W. *The Individual and His Religion.* New York: Macmillan, 1950.

———. "What Units Shall We Employ?" In *Personality and Social Encounter: Selected Essays,* 111–29. Boston: Beacon, 1960.

Beers, Mark H., editor in chief. *The Merck Manual of Medical Information.* 2nd home ed. New York: Simon & Schuster, 2003.

Booth, Wayne C. *A Rhetoric of Irony.* Chicago: University of Chicago Press, 1974.

Breuer, Josef, and Sigmund Freud. *Studies on Hysteria.* New York: Basic Books, 1957.

Bunyan, John. *The Pilgrim's Progress.* New York: Washington Square Press, 1957.

Call, Annie Payson. *As a Matter of Course.* Teddington, UK: Echo Library, 2007.

———. *Power through Repose.* Boston: Roberts Brothers, 1891.

Capps, Donald. *Agents of Hope: A Pastoral Psychology.* Eugene, OR: Wipf & Stock, 2001.

———. "Alzheimer's Disease and the Loss of Self." *The Journal of Pastoral Care & Counseling* 62 (2008) 19–28.

———. *At Home in the World: A Study in Psychoanalysis, Religion, and Art.* Eugene, OR: Cascade Books, 2013.

———. "Charlie." *Literary Cavalcade* 9 (1957) 14–15.

———. *The Decades of Life: A Guide to Human Development.* Louisville: Westminster John Knox, 2008.

———. "Erik H. Erikson's Psychological Portrait of Jesus: Jesus as Numinous Presence." In *Psychology and the Bible: A New Way to Read the Scriptures,* edited by J. Harold Ellens and Wayne G. Rollins, 4:163–208. 4 vols. Praeger Perspectives. Westport, CT: Praeger, 2004.

———. *Laughter Ever After: Ministry of Good Humor.* Eugene, OR: Wipf & Stock, 2014.

———. *Social Phobia: Alleviating Anxiety in an Age of Self-Promotion.* Eugene, OR: Wipf & Stock, 2010.

———. *A Time to Laugh: The Religion of Humor.* New York: Continuum, 2005.

Capps, Donald, and Nathan Carlin. *Living in Limbo: Life in the Midst of Uncertainty.* Eugene, OR: Cascade Books, 2010.

──────. "Methuselah and Company: A Case of Male Envy of Female Longevity." *Pastoral Psychology* 58 (2009) 107–26.

──────. "The Tooth Fairy: Psychological Issues Related to Baby Tooth Loss and Mythological Working Through." *Pastoral Psychology* 63 (2014) 265–80.

Carlin, Nathan, and Donald Capps. "Coming to Terms with Our Regrets." *Journal of Religion and Health* 48 (2009) 224–39.

──────. *100 Years of Happiness: Insights and Findings from the Experts*. Santa Barbara, CA: Praeger, 2012.

Cochran, Sam V., and Fredric E. Rabinowitz. *Men and Depression: Clinical and Empirical Perspectives*. Practical Resources for the Mental Health Professional. San Diego: Academic Press.

Collins, Billy. *The Apple That Astonished Paris*. Fayetteville: University of Arkansas Press, 1988.

Day, Dorothy. *The Long Loneliness: The Autobiography of Dorothy Day*. San Francisco: Harper & Row, 1952.

Disney, Walt. *Snow White and the Seven Dwarfs* (animated film). Hollywood: Disney Studios, 1937.

Dormandy, Thomas. *Old Masters: Great Artists in Old Age*. London: Hambledon and London, 2000.

Duemer, Joseph, and Jim Simmerman, eds. *Dog Music: Poetry about Dogs*. New York: St. Martin's, 1996.

Dworkin, Ronald W. *Artificial Happiness: The Dark Side of the New Happy Class*. New York: Carroll & Graf, 2006.

Dykstra, Robert C., ed. *Images of Pastoral Care: Classic Readings*. St. Louis: Chalice, 2005.

Dykstra, Robert C., et al. *The Faith and Friendships of Teenage Boys*. Louisville: Westminster John Knox, 2012.

Erikson, Erik H. *Childhood and Society*. New York: Norton, 1950.

──────. *Childhood and Society*. 2nd ed., rev. and enl. New York: Norton, 1963.

──────. "The Galilean Sayings and the Sense of 'I.'" *Yale Review* 70 (1981) 321–62.

──────. "Human Strength and the Cycle of Generations." In *Insight and Responsibility*, 107–57. New York: Norton, 1964.

──────. *Identity and the Life Cycle: Selected Papers*. Psychological Issues 1. New York: International Universities Press, 1959.

──────. *Identity, Youth, and Crisis*. New York: Norton, 1968.

──────. *Insight and Responsibility: Lectures on the Psychological Implications of Psychoanalytic Insight*. New York: Norton, 1964.

──────. *The Life Cycle Completed*. New York: Norton, 1982.

──────. "On the Nature of Clinical Evidence." In *Insight and Responsibility*, 47–80. New York: Norton, 1964.

──────. "Psychoanalytic Reflections on Einstein's Centenary." In *Albert Einstein: Historical and Cultural Perspectives*, edited by Gerald Holton and Yehuda Elkana, 151–73. Princeton: Princeton University Press, 1982.

──────. "Reflections on Dr. Borg's Life Cycle." In *Adulthood: Essays*, edited by Erik H. Erikson, 1–31. New York: Norton, 1978.

──────. "Studies in the Interpretation of Play: Clinical Observation of Play Disruption of Young Children." In *A Way of Looking at Things: Selected Papers from 1930 to 1980*, edited by Stephen Schlein, 139–236. New York: Norton, 1987.

———. *Toys and Reasons: Stages in the Ritualization of Experience.* New York: Norton, 1977.

Erikson, Erik H., and Joan M. Erikson. *The Life Cycle Completed: Extended Version.* New York: Norton, 1997.

Erikson, Erik H., et al. *Vital Involvement in Old Age.* New York: Norton, 1986.

Erikson, Joan M. *Wisdom and the Senses: The Way of Creativity.* New York: Norton, 1988.

Fletcher, Horace. *Happiness as Found in Forethought Minus Fearthought.* Menticulture Series 2. Chicago: Kindergarten Literature, 1898.

———. *Menticulture, or, The A-B-C of True Living.* Chicago: McClurg, 1896.

Freud, Sigmund. "The Acquisition of Power over Fire." In *Character and Culture,* edited by Philip Rieff, 294–300. Collected Papers of Sigmund Freud 9. New York: Collier, 1963.

———. *An Autobiographical Study.* Translated by James Strachey. New York: Norton, 1952.

———. *Beyond the Pleasure Principle: A Study of the Death Instinct in Human Behavior.* Translated by James Strachey. Bantam Classics. New York: Bantam, 1959.

———. *Civilization and Its Discontents.* Translated and edited by James Strachey. New York: Norton, 1989.

———. "The Economic Problem of Masochism." In *General Psychological Theory: Papers on Metapsychology,* edited by Philip Rieff, 190–201. Collected Papers of Sigmund Freud 6. New York: Collier, 1963.

———. "Humor." In *Character and Culture,* edited by Philip Rieff, 263–69. Collected Papers of Sigmund Freud 9. New York: Collier, 1963.

———. *Inhibitions, Symptoms, and Anxiety.* Translated by Alix Strachey. Revised and edited by James Strachey. The Standard Edition of the Complete Psychological Works of Sigmund Freud. New York: Norton, 1989.

———. *Jokes and Their Relation to the Unconscious.* Translated by James Strachey. New York: Norton, 1960.

———. *Leonardo da Vinci and a Memory of His Childhood.* New York: Norton, 1964.

———. "Reflections upon War and Death." In *Character and Culture,* edited by Philip Rieff, 107–33. Collected Papers of Sigmund Freud 9. New York: Collier, 1963.

Friedman, Lawrence J. *Menninger: The Family and the Clinic.* New York: Knopf, 1990.

Furman, Ben, and Tapani Ahola. *Solution Talk: Hosting Therapeutic Conversations.* New York: Norton.

Gay, Peter. *Freud: A Life for Our Times.* New York: Norton, 1988.

Greenberg, Jeff, et al. "Aging: Denying the Face of the Future." In *Ageism: Stereotyping and Prejudice against Older Persons,* edited by Todd D. Nelson, 27–48. Cambridge: MIT Press, 2004.

Grimm, Jacob, and Wilhelm Grimm. *The Complete Grimm's Fairy Tales.* New York: Pantheon, 1944.

Hempel, Amy, and Jim Shepard, eds. *Unleashed: Poems by Writers' Dogs.* New York: Three Rivers Press, 1995.

Hillman, James. "Peaks and Vales: The Soul/Spirit Distinction as Basis for the Difference between Psychology and Spiritual Discipline." In *Puer Papers,* edited by James Hillman et al., 54–74. Irving, TX: Spring, 1979.

———. *Re-visioning Psychology.* New York: Harper & Row, 1975.

Housdon, Roger. "One Life, One Season." *AARP* July/August, 2003.

James, William. "The Energies of Men." In *Writings, 1902–1910*, edited by Bruce Kuklick, 1223–41. The Library of America 38. New York: Literary Classics of the United States, distributed by Viking, 1987.

———. "The Gospel of Relaxation." In *Writings 1878–1899*, edited by Gerald E. Myers, 825–840. The Library of America 58. New York: Literary Classics of the United States, distributed by Viking, 1992.

———. *Pragmatism*. Great Books in Philosophy. Buffalo: Prometheus, 1991.

———. *The Principles of Psychology*, vol. 1. New York: Dover, 1950.

———. *The Varieties of Religious Experience*. In *Writings 1902–1910*, edited by Bruce Kuklick, 1–477. The Library of America 38. New York: The Library of America, 1987.

———. "What Is an Emotion?" *Mind* 9 (1885) 188–205.

———. *The Will to Believe*. In *Writings 1878–1899*, edited by Gerald E. Myers, 457–79. The Library of America 58. New York: Literary Classics of the United States, distributed by Viking, 1992.

———. *Writings 1878–1899*. Edited by Gerald E. Myers. Library of America 58. New York: Literary Classics of the United States, distributed by Viking, 1992.

———. *Writings 1902–1910*. Edited by Bruce Kuklick. The Library of America 38. New York: The Library of America, 1987.

Jastrow, Morris, Jr. "The Liver as the Seat of the Soul" (1912). In *Studies in the History of Religions*, edited by David Gordon Lyon and George Foot Moore, 143–68. New York: Macmillan, 1912.

Johns, Elizabeth. *Thomas Eakins: The Heroism of Modern Life*. Princeton: Princeton University Press, 1983.

Johnson, James Weldon. *God's Trombones: Seven Negro Sermons in Verse*. Penguin Poets. New York: Penguin, 1976.

Kallir, Jane. *Grandma Moses, The Artist behind the Myth*. New York: Clarkson N. Potter, 1982.

Kaufman, Sharon R. *The Ageless Self: Sources of Meaning in Late Life*. Life Course Studies. Madison: University of Wisconsin Press, 1986.

Kenyon, Jane. *Collected Poems*. Saint Paul: Graywolf, 2005

Kunitz, Stanley. *The Collected Poems*. New York: Norton, 2000.

Lacan, Jacques. "The Mirror Stage as Formative of the Function of the I as Revealed in Psychoanalytic Experience." In *Écrits: A Selection*, 1–7. New York: Norton, 1977.

Lawrence, of the Resurrection, Brother. *The Practice of the Presence of God: The Best Rule of the Holy Life*. New York: Revell, 1895.

Le Goff, Jacques. *The Birth of Purgatory*. Chicago: University of Chicago Press, 1984.

Levertov, Denise. *Selected Poems*, with a preface by Robert Creeley. Edited, with an afterword by Paul A. Lacey. New York: New Directions, 2002.

Levinson, Daniel J., in collaboration with Judy D. Levinson. *The Seasons of a Woman's Life*. New York: Knopf, 1996.

Levinson, Daniel J., et al. *The Seasons of a Man's Life*. New York: Knopf, 1978.

Lynch, William F. *Images of Hope: Imagination as Healer of the Hopeless*. New York: Mentor-Omega, 1965.

Marmor, Michael F., and James G. Ravin. *The Artist's Eyes: Vision and the History of Art*. New York: Abrams, 2009.

Menninger, Karl A., with the collaboration of Jeanetta Lyle Menninger. *Love against Hate*. New York: Harcourt, Brace, 1942.

————. *Man against Himself*. New York: Harcourt, Brace, 1938.

————. *The Vital Balance: The Life Process in Mental Health and Illness*, with Martin Mayman and Paul Pruyser. New York: Viking, 1963.

Murphy, Gardner. *Historical Introduction to Modern Psychology*. Rev. ed. New York: Harcourt, Brace & World, 1949.

Nouwen, Henri J. M. *The Wounded Healer: Ministry in Contemporary Society*. New York: Image, 1972.

Prebble, Stuart. *Grumpy Old Men: The Official Handbook*. London: BBC Books, 2006.

Pruyser, Paul W. "Aging: Downward, Upward, or Forward?" *Pastoral Psychology* 24 (1975) 102–18.

————. *Between Belief and Unbelief*. New York: Harper & Row, 1974.

————. "Creativity in Aging Persons." *Bulletin of the Menninger Clinic* 51 (1987) 425–35.

————. *A Dynamic Psychology of Religion*. New York: Harper & Row, 1968.

————. "An Essay on Creativity." *Bulletin of the Menninger Clinic* 43 (1979) 294–353.

————. *The Minister as Diagnostician: Personal Problems in Pastoral Perspective*. Philadelphia: Westminster, 1976.

————. *The Play of the Imagination: Towards a Psychoanalysis of Culture*. New York: International Universities Press, 1983.

————. "Where Do We Go From Here? Scenarios for the Psychology of Religion." *Journal for the Scientific Study of Religion* 26 (1987) 173–81.

Rennison, Nick. *Freud & Psychoanalysis*. Pocket Essential. North Pomfret, VT: Pocket Essentials, 2001.

Rotenberg, Mordechai. "The 'Midrash' and Biographic Rehabilitation." *Journal for the Scientific Study of Religion* 25 (1986) 41–55.

Rothman, Rodney. *Early Bird: A Memoir of Premature Retirement*. New York: Simon & Schuster, 2005.

Ryken, Leland. *Words of Delight: A Literary Introduction to the Bible*. 2nd ed. Grand Rapids: Baker, 1992.

Santayana, George. *The Sense of Beauty*. New York: Dover, 1955.

Scott, Donald. *The Psychology of Fire*. New York: Scribner, 1974.

Selzer, Richard. *Mortal Lessons: Notes on the Art of Surgery*. New York: Simon & Schuster, 1974.

Shakespeare, William. *As You Like It*. Edited by Frances E. Dolan. New York: Penguin, 2000.

————. *The Complete Works*. Edited by G. B. Harrison. New York: Harcourt, Brace & World, 1948.

Simon, Linda. *Genuine Reality: A Life of William James*. New York: Harcourt, Brace, 1998.

Smith, Hannah Whitall. *A Christian's Secret to a Happy Life*. New Kensington, PA: Whitaker House, 2005.

Stafford, William. *The Way It Is: New & Selected Poems*. St. Paul: Graywolf, 1998.

Tapper, Albert, and Peter Press. *A Minister, a Priest, and a Rabbi*. Kansas City: McMeel, 2000.

Terkel, Studs. *Working: People Talk about What They Do All Day and How They Feel about What They Do*. New York: Pantheon, 1974.

Timmerman, John H. *Jane Kenyon: A Literary Life*. Grand Rapids: Eerdmans, 2002.

Trevor-Roper, Patrick. *The World through Blunted Sight: An Inquiry into the Influence of Defective Vision on Art and Character.* Rev. ed. London: Penguin, 1988.

Webber, Marilyn Carlson, and William D. Webber. *How to Become a Sweet Old Lady Instead of a Grumpy Old Grouch.* Grand Rapids: Zondervan, 1996.

Wessman, Alden E., and David F. Ricks. *Mood and Personality.* New York: Holt, Rinehart and Winston, 1966.

Whitman, Walt. *Selected Poems.* New York: Gramercy, 1992.

Weyn, Suzanne. *Walt Disney's Classic Snow White and the Seven Dwarfs.* New York: Scholastic, 1987.

Wikipedia. Grimms Fairy Tales. http://en.wikipedia.org/wiki/Grimms_fairy_tales/.

Wikipedia. *Snow White and the Seven Dwarfs (1937 Film).* http://en.wikipedia.org/wiki/Snow_White_and_the_Seven_Dwarfs_(1937_film).

Wilson, Eric. G. *Against Happiness: In Praise of Melancholy.* New York: Farrar, Straus & Giroux, 2008.

Winnicott, David W. *Home Is Where We Start From: Essays by a Psychoanalyst.* New York: Norton, 1986.

———. *Playing and Reality.* New York: Routledge, 1982.

———. "Transitional Objects and Transitional Phenomena: A Study of the First Not-me Possession." *International Journal of Psychoanalysis* 34 (1953) 89–97.

Wyer, Carol E. *How not to Murder Your Grumpy.* London: Safkhet, 2013.

Yeats, William Butler. *Selected Poetry.* Edited by A. Norman Jeffares. St. Martin's Library. London: Macmillan, 1962.

Index

James, William (*continued*)
  and Lange-James theory of
    emotions, 118–20
  and moral tensions, 131
  and not caring, 128–29, 141
  personal history of, 116–17
  and power of ideas, 134–37
  and religion, 129–30
  and self-forgetfulness, 126–29
  and Sigmund Freud, 119–20,
    126
  and "The Energies of Men," xv,
    xviii, 117, 131–38
  and "The Gospel of Relaxation,"
    117–31
Jesus,
  calming the storm, 139–40
  and non-resistance, 166–67
  Also see Christ
Johnson, James Weldon, 174–75
Johns, Elizabeth, 109
joking, 16
  and irony, 9–10
  See also humor
joy, 54, 117
Jung, C. G., 77

Kallir, Jane, xix, 104
Kallir, Otto, 104
Kaufman, Sharon, 12–13
Kenyon, Jane, 170–71
Kivnick, Helen O., 46–49
Kunitz, Stanley, 61–62

Lacan, Jacques, 96
  and self-discovery, 96
Lange, Carl, 118
Leonardo da Vinci, 104–5
Levertov, Denise, 172
Levinson, Daniel J.
  and mentor relationship, 21–26
life process, 69
limbo, 17
liver
  as seat of passions, 7
  as locus of the soul, 146
living in the present, 76–77

loneliness
  and creativity, 174–75
  and minister, xviii, 171–72
  and older adulthood, xviii, 172
longevity, 85
Lorain, Claude, 107

macular degeneration, 105–6
Marmor, Michael E., 105–6
maturational process, 73
memory reorganization, 96–97
Menninger, Karl
  and death instinct, 80–81
  and prison reform, 79
  the vital balance, 80–81, 86
mental energy, 131–33
release of, 133–37
mental hygiene, 117–18
mentor
  as transitional figure, 23–27
  relationship, 21–26
  symbolic, 24–25
  younger self as, 26–27
Michelangelo, 104, 107–8
ministry
  and older adults, xviii,169,
    172–73
mood, 116
  changes in, xviii, 142–46
  defined as, 143
  eradication of negative, 164–67
  grumpy, 145
  happy, 145
  and personality, 147–48
moral tensions, 130
Moses, Anna Mary Robertson
  ("Grandma"), xviii–xix, 103
mystical faculties, 132

Noah, xix
Nouwen, Henri, xviii, 172–73

object relations
  loss of, 72
oedipal tensions and conflicts, 95
O'Keefe, Georgia, 105–6

Made in the USA
Middletown, DE
27 January 2022

59722604R00125